Know Your
Own
POWER

Know Your Own

POWER

Inspiration, Motivation and Practical Tools For Life

Dr Radha Modgil

yellow
kite

First published in Great Britain in 2022 by Yellow Kite
An imprint of Hodder & Stoughton
An Hachette UK company

This paperback edition published in 2023

1

A CIP catalogue record for this title is available
from the British Library

Paperback ISBN 978 1 529 36721 8
eBook ISBN 978 1 529 36719 5

Typeset in Odile by Goldust Design

Printed and bound in Great Britain by Clays Ltd, Elcograf S.p.A.

Hodder & Stoughton policy is to use papers that are natural,
renewable and recyclable products and made from wood grown
in sustainable forests. The logging and manufacturing
processes are expected to conform to the environmental
regulations of the country of origin.

Yellow Kite
Hodder & Stoughton Ltd
Carmelite House
50 Victoria Embankment
London EC4Y 0DZ

www.yellowkitebooks.co.uk

ABOUT THE AUTHOR

Dr Radha Modgil is an NHS GP, a television, radio and podcast broadcaster and author on a mission to bring about positive change in the world and empower people.

Radha is the medical expert for both BBC Radio 1's daytime show, *Life Hacks*, and BBC 5 Live's *Mental Health Clinic*, and was the presenter of the CBeebies show, *Feeling Better*, which highlighted the importance of talking to young children about their feelings. She also appeared as the medical expert for *The Sex Education Show* on Channel 4 and *Make My Body Younger* on BBC Three. She is a weekly columnist for *The i* Newspaper, writing about how we can all live our best lives.

Radha is passionate about helping people feel that they are not alone in their struggles and challenges they face. She's worked on several wellbeing campaigns with BBC Children in Need, Public Health England, MIND and the British Red Cross and is also an ambassador for the National Academy for Social Prescribing, the Youth Sports Trust, National Careers Week and the mental health charity We Are Beyond.

This book is dedicated to anyone who has
ever felt powerless or alone. May you find
your power once again.

CONTENTS

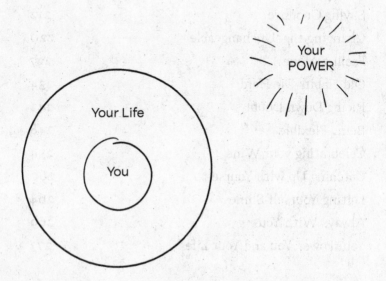

YOUR LIFE, YOU AND YOUR POWER

There is nothing more powerful than the power
you have and hold inside yourself
When you realise this, you are able to get through
something, face anything and change everything

Life happens. We face obstacles, setbacks and crises. Sometimes life can feel harsh, painful, unfair and over-whelming. It hits hard.

But life doesn't have to happen *to* us. It can happen around us. It can happen alongside us. It can happen within us. And, most importantly, *we* can happen to *it*.

We don't have to be silent, powerless observers of our lives. Each and every one of us has an indescribable, infinite and intelligent power inside us that we can use to not only get through life's crises, challenges and changes, but to become more of who we truly are through the process and to create the life that we were born to live.

We can overcome to become.

Do you have the courage to believe that you have power over your life? To find that power, to see it, to use it and to be it?

Do you have the courage to change your life?

I know what it feels like to have life crash down around you, not just once but many times. I know what it's like to feel lost and powerless, and then to try to salvage any pieces you can and be expected to carry on as 'normal' in the midst of all the rubble. And I know you do, too. We all experience tough times, heartbreaking pain, life-changing loss and overwhelming sadness. We all get lost, distracted, confused and hurt.

What we don't always see, though, is that right in the middle of all of this, life is offering something precious; something that, in the long run, will help us. Life offers us the chance to find our power. We get presented with life lessons to learn, opportunities to understand ourselves more and the chance to become the authority in our own lives. We get an insight as to how we can shine out there in the world and an idea about why we are here on this earth. If we see these lessons, if we accept them and if we use them, then we find our power - our power to get through anything and be OK.

And then we don't feel so scared, so lost, so anxious and so abandoned. We can approach life with more confidence, more understanding and more trust. Because we can trust that power inside us.

I wrote this book because I don't want anyone to be

alone in their struggles. I don't want anyone to feel alone in their challenges. I don't want anyone to think they are alone in trying to change something in their lives.

I want you to know that you *can* change things, that things can be different for you and that you absolutely deserve them to be. I want you to know that, whatever happens, you have this power inside of you, and you can do anything you want when you use it. This is not about 'fixing' or 'changing' yourself because there is 'something wrong' with you, and it's not about living a 'perfect' life. There is nothing to 'fix' – you are incredible and more than enough just as you are – and there is nothing 'wrong' with you.

This is about empowering you to make changes in your life that you want to make. This is about helping you to be more of who you are without all the 'stuff' we are told to be. Mostly it's about supporting you to make decisions, choices and changes from a place of knowing your own unique, authentic power.

I know that platitudes and clichés are irritating and useless, so I've created a book that really puts power in your hands. It's full of practical tips, everyday, relatable examples and helpful insights that I have gained through my life to help you realise what you can do, exactly how you could do it and why it might help. As you read, you will come across insights in the words and inspiration in the quotes. Each chapter focuses on a tangible step, an emotional stage or a practical tool. Every chapter contains a different gift that you are being offered by whatever you are going through. Your power is made up of these gifts. And, once accepted, each gift can help you find your power.

Just as your journey of rediscovering your power will take time and go through different phases and stages, so this book has been written to help take you along that path of moving from experiencing a crisis in life, to facing the challenges and eventually moving forward by changing things. Pace yourself and be gentle with your individual process. At any point, at any stage and in any moment you can dip in and out of the book and find your way again. I hope this book will be your best friend,

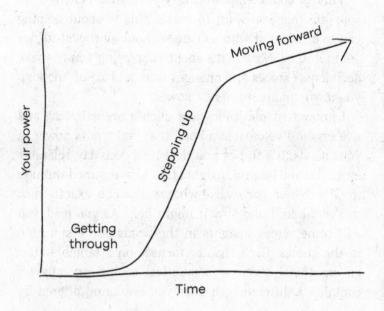

your constant companion, your wisest counsel and most trustworthy guide. I hope it can inspire and motivate you to finally go looking for your power, find it, dust it off and let it show you what it can do for you.

Once discovered, this power can never leave you, you will never be without it and you will never be alone. You will be able to rely on it, to trust it and know that it can help you, whatever life brings.

When the next storm hits, you can turn to face it, look it straight in the eye and quietly but confidently whisper, 'You have no power over me... anymore.'

Your Power

You can get through this

However hard, however difficult,
however dark things seem

There is always a light inside you
that wants to shine through

That light is the power you hold
within

And it wants to help you

Let it dazzle you again

STEP 1

Days add up to weeks
Weeks add up to months
And months to a way forward
So, for now, focus on one day at a time
You will get through this

When life hits and hits hard, you have the ability, the capacity and the capability to get through. I know it doesn't feel like that right now. I know you are struggling and I know you are tired.

But let me remind you of one thing: you already have the power within you to get through this. You just have to understand what that power looks like, what it practically translates into and how to find it again, and I'm going to help you do just that.

WARNING SIGNS

A crisis has two sides to it
The one that confronts us first and is,
unfortunately, all too easy to see – it feels
terrifying and dark
And the one that it takes more willingness and
courage to find – a necessity, an opportunity,
a rare gift
You get to choose which one you focus on

Life is like an alarm clock - it's just doing its best to try to wake us up. Are you still asleep? Or are you ready to wake up?

Some crises happen out of the blue, when we least expect them - we lose our job, we lose someone we love, we have to move away from everything we know, our relationship breaks down, our family falls apart, we become unwell, we experience financial hardship - and we don't have the opportunity to act early to try to stop them in their tracks.

But with those setbacks that happen more gradually, there will have been warning signs or repeated signals trying to help us realise that we need to pay attention or change something fast to avoid the situation moving into the life crisis zone. Maybe that is recurrent arguments with a friend, feeling more alone in your relationship or a family dynamic that keeps replaying every summer holiday or Christmas. Maybe it's your boss always calling you into their office just as you're ready to leave or you feeling like you are not looking after yourself enough. Or perhaps you just generally feel lost and unsure about where your life is going. I've definitely ignored warning signs before. Deep down, if we are being honest, most of us have known for a long time that things aren't right. But we just carry on going on our pre-planned route, scared of stopping and re-routing or taking a diversion for fear we might get lost. And because we want things our way. However, in just frantically carrying on, we are already lost. And we only get more lost.

When the comfort of the familiar becomes more and more painful and this hurt outweighs the scariness of the unfamiliar; when we outgrow our need to stay in our comfort zone; and when our need to live more authentically is finally more of a pull factor, we start to take notice. And this is an important step in discovering the very nature of the power that we all hold inside.

Life is not some nasty playground bully trying to hurt us; it's just trying to get our attention. It is trying to help us. It is telling us that something is not right and warning us that, unless we change something, a potential crisis is on its way. It is trying to make us make a change to prevent a major life upheaval.

What Do Warning Signs Look or Feel Like?

> Feeling lost.

> Recurring events happening in your life, repeating dynamics in relationships or patterns of behaviour.

> Living your life like a tick box – according to what others want.

> Realising that what you thought would bring you joy just doesn't.

> Feeling like you are just going through the motions, because you 'should'.

> Becoming less clear about why you are doing things.

> Starting to make excuses to yourself and other people for why things are as they are rather than being honest with yourself.

> ❯ Trying to convince yourself that something will just change or that it is not a problem.

> ❯ Finding it harder to be who you truly are and communicating your needs less.

> ❯ Putting yourself last and feeling obliged to do things you don't want to do.

> ❯ Distracting yourself by being overly busy.

> ❯ Pretending to yourself that you are happy.

Listen to these warning signs. They can save you a lot of time, emotional energy and heartache. They can prevent difficult life situations or inconveniences from gaining momentum and hurtling you into a crisis situation. They can stop you from getting in deeper.

Let's take the example of a relationship ending. In most cases, and if we are all being honest, there will have been plenty of warning signs for a long while before the relationship actually ends. It is just that we don't necessarily spot them, or we don't want to. Maybe we are talking less to each other, not spending much time together, having more arguments, feeling more alone and less understood. Maybe we have become less of ourselves and more of the other person. I am not saying that if we acted on these warning signs sooner the relationship would have been saved, but heeding the warning signs means less emotional heartache and energy, less hurt. And it shows us that this noticing is a power we can develop.

The signs are always there to see
The message is always there to hear
The signals are always there to be heeded
And the truth is held in each

It is never too late. Even if you are in deep, it's better to extricate yourself now than to let yourself sink any deeper. **Listen, hear, notice, act and sort it.** Don't sit in it any longer. Even if it feels more comfortable because it is familiar or you have invested a lot into it, don't ignore things anymore.

REALISING

To get clearer is handy
To know more is useful
To understand is helpful
But to realise is everything

I will never forget that moment of 'realising' that the relationship I was in was just not right. And when it hit me, it hit hard - a lurching feeling in my stomach, my heart beating faster and the feeling of loneliness with absolutely nowhere to go. I realised that things weren't working, that things were not going to go the way I had thought or hoped, no matter how much I wanted or tried to make them.

That realising hurt. Not just because it meant the loss of a dream and what I thought I wanted, but also because it meant I would have to now face the even more difficult challenge of facing up to the breakdown of that relationship. I would have to face what was actually going on and deal with all the difficult feelings and all that hurt.

If you are lucky, this realising just hits one area of your life at a time. But frequently it hits more than one all at once - and takes you on the wildest dodgem ride you have ever been on; getting hit from all sides and coming off it tottering, disorientated and trying to regain your balance. You know - that realisation that knocks you sideways when you recognise that not only is your family slowly falling apart, but also that you just can't take your horrendous job anymore and that you are trapped in a life that doesn't feel like yours. It's all too much all at once.

Eventually, like hide-and-seek, life finds you, gives you a tap on the shoulder and says, 'Got you'. You can't run and you can't hide... any more. And although it is not pleasant, it's helpful to recognise that we now need to realise.

Unfortunately, it often takes a crisis to make us stop and realise. Once we do, though, there is something else we can realise - that tied up in all that reality and hurt and fear is a gift, an opportunity to change something, to transform a situation into something that is more authentic and step into a place where we can really create the life we want.

When life hits hard, we have a choice to stay floored on the ground or to realise the fight is not over and to struggle to our feet once again. We have some fight still left in us. Fight that will reclaim our true selves. That's where our power lies.

That is why realising needs to happen. And, if we get comfortable with our power to realise, we save ourselves a lot of hassle, we avoid riding the emotional dodgems and we lessen the heartache.

How do you realise?

MAKE TIME

Life gets busy. It becomes automatic. We allow ourselves on to an escalator and our life situation becomes so 'normal' that eventually we don't even notice that that escalator is taking us to the wrong floor. We can use work and 'being busy' as a useful distraction and an excuse to avoid realising. Slow down, stop and reflect. Make time every single day for some space away from doing, doing, doing. Go for a long cycle, feel the sun on your face, shuffle through leaves on the ground, have a bath, sit and drink a cup of tea slowly. Do the things you used to do on your long summer holidays from school, when you felt you had all the time in the world. Time and space will help you to realise what is actually going on.

NOTICE HOW YOU FEEL

Hurt and pain are not nice, but they are part of life and we can't avoid them. We suffer even more when we ignore our feelings. Instead of turning down the volume on your feelings, turn down the noise from the outside world and other people's opinions. Listen to what your feelings are telling you. They are there for a reason and can help you realise if you just let them. These feelings can be painful, but you can choose not to suffer in the long term by realising the truth of a situation. Denial and pushing down uncomfortable feelings just doesn't work. Dig deep, be courageous, ask for help and support. **Show yourself that you care about yourself, and let your feelings be felt.**

Stepping out of denial is the most terrifying
thing you can do
And the most courageous
It frees you, it empowers you and it shapes you
Better to be terrified temporarily, than to live half
a life permanently

TRANSFORM YOUR FEELINGS INTO SOMETHING TANGIBLE

Write down your feelings and your thoughts to help you see the situation for what it is. Just like tidying up a room helps you find what you need to find, tipping out all your thoughts and feelings on to a page helps you realise what you need to realise.

FIND A SOUNDING BOARD

Other people can help us realise. They act like a mirror reflecting our truth back to us and, like a sounding board, amplify the truth of what we speak. They can ask us questions that, deep down, we knew we should have asked ourselves and could have answered a long time ago. But that's OK - everything happens at the right time and we all realise things at the right time for us; when we have grown enough to be able to. Choose friends who really listen, who allow you to express yourself and who don't offer their opinion unless you ask. Avoid those who project their opinions on to you or who tell you what to do, or you will get even more lost. Sometimes the right words from someone who cares about you spoken at exactly the right moment are the very thing that helps you realise. Pay attention to the people you meet, the music that comes on the radio and the books that you read - they may hold the exact words that you need to hear.

FOCUS ON THE NOW

Realising forces us to change something in the present and then face up to an uncertain future. When that future is totally unknown, fear creeps in like an unwanted blast of cold air on a sunny day and makes us shiver and run for cover. Fear can paralyse us and is a major reason we delay realising. Breathe and focus on the now – what you are certain of right now – one step at a time. The future will work itself out in time. Have faith.

It takes incredible courage to realise. It is never easy. **Once you 'realise', there is no going back, even if you don't know where on earth you are going.**

Realising ignites the power inside us to change things up. It's like rocket fuel and helps us move up and out of those scary and lost-feeling moments on a new trajectory and a new path. **It is only by us realising that we don't want something anymore, that we realise what we do want.**

WHEN THINGS FALL APART

When the ground gets shaken beneath your feet
When the walls start to collapse around you
When the sun disappears behind the clouds
When the nights seem longer than the days
You have the power inside of you to hold firm

I have never been a natural baker. Don't get me wrong, I have always got top marks for taste, but absolutely the opposite for 'presentation'; there have been so many moments when I've removed a cake from its tin, hoping that it will stay in one piece - holding my breath, thinking about all that effort and time I've put in - only to be confronted with the whole thing falling apart. After several deluded attempts to put it back together so no one notices, I've had to accept it. And it's the same with life; often I have had to accept that sometimes, no matter what I do, just like my cake, all my efforts have literally crumbled right in front of my eyes.

When everything that you have worked so hard for, struggled for and painstakingly held together through thick and thin just unravels, it has more far-reaching consequences than my 'deconstructed' cake. In its wake it leaves behind a trail of destruction, painful remnants of broken dreams and a once-believed-in future. We find it heart-wrenchingly hard to accept. For a while, we try to take pieces of it and stick it back together, before we have to accept it is unsalvageable. Perhaps we have been struggling in a job that is slowly but surely draining us of all our enthusiasm and has started causing huge stress. We keep at it, hoping that it will just 'get better' one day, while our health and well-being slowly deteriorate, and our personal lives gradually fall apart because of it. I think all of us, myself included, have tried for weeks, months or even years trying to 'stick' a relationship that is already clearly broken back together, only to realise that it is not going to work and that all we are doing is wasting our time and emotional energy.

When things fall apart, we feel a sense of impending loss. Often these losses can be silent ones – not things that we had and then lost, but rather things that we desperately wanted and yet never had, like a desire to have a family that was never realised or a career in a particular field that was never possible for practical reasons. These

When Things Are Going Down the Drain

> Surround yourself with things that feel safe, familiar and constant.

> Write your thoughts down, let your feelings out.

> Comfort yourself as much as you can. Let those who love you do the same.

> Create something to look forward to every single day - however small.

> Control what you can. Let go of what you can't. Be wise.

losses are just as painful and need to be respected as such. Now these dreams appear to have slipped through our fingers, just like that.

Despite all this, take some solace. My crumbled cake still got full marks for how it tasted. **In the wake of destruction, there is still a lot we can salvage and so much we can still hold on to.**

How do you salvage what you can?

ACCEPT IT

The more you try to control and hang on to something, the less controllable it becomes and the more likely it will slip through your fingers. Acceptance brings its own gift too - one of liberation. When things fall apart, we are free. And freedom brings peace. No more trying, no more effort, no more exhausting excuses. The illusion of control disappears. And control is always an illusion, even though none of us wants to believe this. The only thing we can control is ourselves. Once you accept what has happened and stop trying to hold all the disjointed pieces together, you have stopped pretending. And that means new things can be created.

Your real power lies in letting go
Of what is no longer of you
Of what is no longer with you
Of what is no longer for you

CONNECT WITH THE FAMILIAR

When everything falls apart, we feel like the ground has been pulled from beneath our feet. We need to find some of those remaining foundation stones, those constants that have not changed. It might be your family or your friends; it might be your favourite soap opera, your dog or your gym class every Tuesday. Find some normality, some sense of familiar routine, some reassuring moments in your day and in your week to help you know that you are not completely lost. You are not completely ungrounded. **Use those constant things to steady yourself until you find your balance and regroup.**

LET GO, BUT DON'T GIVE UP

One obstacle to accepting that things have fallen apart is the fear that, in doing so, it means we are giving up on our dreams. It does not mean this at all. Just because it is not now, doesn't mean it will never be. In fact, it means the exact opposite. Once we let go, we are free to find another way to reach our dreams, or to find another dream altogether that may be more aligned with who we are.

Find the Gift

Ask yourself:

> Is there anything positive you can find that has come out of the crisis? Something that you could not have foreseen?

> What are you learning about yourself?

> What life lessons are you learning?

> What can you be proud of?

> Who has really been there for you?

> What would have happened long term if you had just carried on with how things were?

> How would you have felt about that?

DEAL WITH THE LIFE ADMIN

There are going to be tangible changes and practical problems to sort out when things fall apart. Maybe it is moving home, maybe it is dividing up friendship groups, maybe it is about reviewing finances or having to drop round your ex-partner's socks that they left at yours. It is tempting to ignore these things and bury your head in the sand, but, if you do, they will likely get worse and cause an even bigger emotional hangover. Spend time dealing with the practical bits sooner rather than later. Ask friends and family to help if you have little emotional reserve to deal with it all. Clearing the practicalities relieves that sense of immediate pressure. Once done, you can focus on yourself, hibernate from the world for a bit and work on healing, mentally and emotionally.

SEE THE BIGGER PICTURE

Trusting there is a reason for all this to happen is a hard ask when everything falls apart. But you have a better chance of getting through this if you can. Try to trust that things will be OK in the end. It is a tool to help you get through this awful period and, given time, you will probably be able to look back and actually believe it. What would your best friend say to you? How would you speak to a little child if they needed reassurance? Speak to yourself in the same way.

Things to Say to Yourself When Things Fall Apart

> 'I am doing the best I can and that's all I can do.'

> 'Things will get better and this will pass.'

> 'I'm doing really well given what I'm facing.'

> 'I know that I matter. I know that I am not alone. I know that I am loved.'

Things have to fall apart in order to come together again; to be created anew and to be built again, but in a different and better way, on stronger, more solid foundations.

TRUSTING YOUR INTUITION

You have the most powerful inner
guidance system
It is called your intuition
Get to know it
Make friends with it
Trust it

'Intuition' is a bit of a grand word, but don't be put off by that. It's not something you attain only after decades of meditation. You have it right now, inside of you. We all do. It's just that we aren't necessarily aware of it, practised in accessing it or comfortable with trusting it. Simply put, it's a sense of something feeling right for you or not. Your intuition is there to protect you. It's an instruction manual to run alongside your bespoke individual life journey. And knowing it is there if you ever need to refer to it is where your power lies in tough times.

No one else's manual is the same as yours and, by that very definition, no one else knows better what to do in your life than you do.

How to tap into your intuition

TUNE IN

When we get creative, our mind settles, distractions quieten down and we can get in touch with ourselves. Find different ways to express yourself: music, art, baking, gardening, moving your body, getting out in nature. Hobbies and self-expression can all help you tune in to your intuition. They turn the loud shouts of the outside world and other people's opinions into a quiet hum of background noise, so you can better hear your inner guidance system.

PRACTISE

A bit like a muscle, the more often you listen to your intuition the more you will get familiar with it and the more quickly and accurately you can respond to it. It's a habit we can all develop - a skill like any other. The more you do it, the more you build trust in yourself that you know what you are doing and the more you can trust your intuition. After all, it is part of you. Your intuition is worth listening to. It's that best friend who is always there for you, if only you let them know you need them.

DON'T WORRY ABOUT SPECIFICS

Even if you don't know exactly what your intuition is telling you or what specifically that feeling is about, it doesn't matter. A general awareness is more than sufficient for now. That will be enough to help guide you in the right direction.

REALISE ITS WORTH

Most of us are never 'taught' about intuition. We are not encouraged to follow it or get familiar with it, and so we don't place a lot of emphasis on it. Once you start to listen to it and follow it, you will realise just how amazing it is. Make a note every time your intuition helps you and guides you, and things work out well for you as a result. Knowing what your intuition can do for you will increase your confidence in it.

Life isn't a baseball game. It's not 'three strikes and you're out'. **Our intuition is always there endlessly pitching balls. We always have another chance at hitting a home run.**

One Thing After Another, After Another

> It's OK to feel it's all a bit too much. It is. But, remember, you are not alone.

> Be proud of what you have got through so far. You're amazing.

> Take a rest and recharge.

> Cry, talk, ask for help, hold on.

> Listen to your intuition – what is it trying to tell you?

> Remember that things never stay the same. So, keep on going. They'll change.

> Never forget that you matter and you will get through this.

WANTING TO GIVE UP

Are you trying to be everything to everybody,
yet no one to yourself?
Why?
You deserve your love as much as they do

'What's the point? I've tried and it just doesn't get me anywhere.'

'Things never, ever work out for me, however hard I try.'

'I'm tired, I have had enough, I'm done.'

Sound familiar? I am sure you have thought or said all of these things, but with a good dose of expletives scattered over the top for full effect. When things fall apart around us it is natural to feel like we just want to give up.

I want to tell you that **you have every right to feel this way.** I hear you. I see you. I feel you. I have been there too. You are tired. You have tried so hard. Your dream hasn't worked out how you wanted it to. You have had enough. You haven't got anything left to give.

All those magazine articles and agony aunt columns

that tell you to get back up straight away or to just think positively and it will all be OK can take a running jump. I'm saying to you that it's OK to feel like giving up. I am not talking about giving up on you, or your mental and physical self-care, or on the absolute practicalities of life, because that will only make things worse. I am talking about just giving up on trying to be perfect, on trying to pick yourself up immediately, on trying to manage or solve everything right now. Just for a little while, give yourself a break from 'being determined' all the time and from 'bouncing back' straight away. You need time to rest, recover, process and heal from what has happened. If you think you have to try to get back out there straight away like nothing has even happened, it is probably coming from a place of fear rather than truth.

I am someone who doesn't like giving up or giving in. But, I have learned to distinguish when my desire to persevere comes from genuine intent, which has a positive, forward energy about it, and when it comes from fear, which has a desperate, clinging and backward-looking sense about it. It doesn't feel peaceful, it doesn't feel calm, and it doesn't work.

Taking a step back temporarily paradoxically opens up new ways for your dreams to happen. Just like a boxer can feel disorientated when they try to get up straight away after a blow, if we try to get up too soon after life has knocked us down, we can make poor decisions. It's tempting to get up straight away because we are anxious, we have lost control and we don't know what is going to happen if we don't. But we need time to feel, to just be. We need to respect and honour what has just happened to us or we will get more lost, more tired and more confused. Never give up on yourself; instead, give up on things that are not helping you.

Things to give up on for now...

TRYING TO
'MOVE THINGS FORWARD'

When we stop pushing and forcing life 'forward', we have to face the reality, start to process what has happened and be with the present. You don't have to 'move on' right now. Just be here right now, where you are. That is hard, it feels uncomfortable and it takes courage, but it is better than struggling in quicksand and just sinking further and faster.

JUDGEMENT

Criticism has a negative energy to it and never, ever brings anything positive. Start to become aware of critical thoughts and feelings, past and present. Just notice them, don't judge. Turn them into something kinder with more positive energy. You more than deserve words of kindness.

STRESSING YOURSELF OUT

You have just had a massive change in your life. The ground beneath your feet has totally shifted. You are exhausted. Rest, sleep, relax and decompress. The pressure needs to be released and to have somewhere to go. Do things that help you release stress - exercise, get outside or listen to music. You need to allow yourself to be.

PUSHING AWAY FEELINGS

Just like it's hard to stop a wave sweeping over the sand, it's even harder to try to push down feelings such as sadness, anxiety and despair. You can't stop the tide. Allow yourself to cry, to weep and to express how you feel. Deep breathe, run, dance, meditate or walk. Your body is an instrument to help you express and process emotions.

WORRYING WHAT OTHER PEOPLE THINK

The only opinion on your life that matters is your own. 'What will they think?', 'What will they say?' Frankly, who cares? 'I have to prove I am OK', 'I have to put up a front.' Why do you need to bother? Giving up on caring what others think not only allows you the freedom to

If Today Feels Overwhelming...

> Put one foot in front of the other.
> Focus on one thing at a time.
> Breathe.
> Remember what you've coped with before.
> Be kind to yourself.
> Just be you.

breathe and to be, it also filters out those who don't have your best interests at heart. A crisis situation is a fast-track route, a high-speed rail line to finding true friends.

Give up on all these things. Show yourself that you are not giving up on yourself.

GETTING THROUGH THE DAYS

Different days, different hours, different
moments all ask something different of us and
from us
But they all have one thing in common
They all require you to be gentle with yourself

When crisis hits, you have to go back to basics. There's
no energy, time or space for frills or fancies.

Just like in any game we play, there are times when we
try to rack up enough points just to get through to the
next round and there are times when we try to achieve
our 'personal best'. Right now, all that is required of you
is just to get through, so take the pressure off yourself.

This strategy has helped me when life has served me
up a super-sized dish of crisis, a side of setbacks and
obstacles galore to wash it all down - just hunker down
and get through today. **Forget thriving. Crisis requires**

you to just get through. **That is more than enough right now.** Creating your own survival toolkit in a crisis is an essential part of this. So, what might it contain?

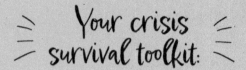

Your crisis survival toolkit:

BASIC PHYSICAL SELF-CARE

Yes, it is dull, but it is necessary. And it feeds into your emotional and mental health. I'm not talking about using a nail file to shape your nails - that's thriving. I'm talking nail clippers - the absolute basics: showering, sleeping and eating regularly. When you practise basic self-care you are showing yourself that you matter, you are worth looking after and that, whatever has happened, you care about yourself. This is an important message that your subconscious will take notice of, appreciate and feed back to your self-esteem. And you need this bolstered up, especially when things have fallen apart around you and you have hit rock bottom.

Small investments in seemingly insignificant
moments of self-care result in big returns
Invest wisely and invest often
You'll be rewarded over and over again

GO THROUGH THE MOTIONS

After crisis hits, sometimes we just have to go
through the motions of getting up, going to work,
coming home again to stream a boxset while we
eat dinner, going to bed and then starting it all over
again the next day. Going through the motions and
having some sense of routine gives us some much-
needed continuity, structure and grounding in our
unfamiliar new world. Routine helps us stabilise
after a shock.

HAVE REALISTIC EXPECTATIONS

You need to catch up with where you are now. In
times gone past you might have had the energy and
the space to thrive, expand and try new things. **But
you need to understand that that time is not now.
It doesn't mean it won't come again.** For now, you
just need to be realistic about what you can handle

and what you can manage. The more you work with where you are right now, without wasting energy on pushing yourself to do things when it is not the right time for you, the more likely and the more quickly you will be able to bounce back.

SET BOUNDARIES

Say no often and with conviction. Reduce contact with those people who stress you out or drain you. Tell people you can't be involved in whatever they are trying to get you to do and that you just need to look after yourself. When we have been through a crisis, sometimes we fall into the trap of telling people who we can't necessarily trust with our precious and delicate feelings, and their response to what we tell them can make us feel so much worse. Choose people you trust to confide in. Do your best to stay away from stressful and unnecessary situations. Feel the fear of loss of friendships or opportunities if you say no, but don't listen because these are often self-sabotaging. Your true friends will stick around.

When It Is All a Bit Too Much

> Turn off your notifications, turn off the news and turn down the noise.

> Pace yourself by your own internal clock, not the outside world's hurtling one.

> Breathe.

> Say no. Work to your own agenda, not other people's.

> Things always get done in the end. Whatever it is, it can wait. 'You' can't.

REFILL AND RECHARGE, THEN RECONNECT

You need to press 'pause' and take some time out or your emotional battery will overheat and run down entirely. Think about what brings you joy, what makes you feel better, what helps you forget for a while. Do these things regularly to recharge your battery and then 'reconnect' to the outside world at the right time for you.

Knowing that you matter is the fail-safe that helps you get through the days. Think of it like an electrical circuit breaker. That circuit will trip when it needs to in order to keep you safe. Caring about yourself and yourself first does exactly the same. **Nothing will get better unless you start realising your inherent self-worth.**

Focus on surviving – just getting through each day – until the next day becomes that 'one day' that you have waited for for so long. That day when things start to feel a bit lighter and you start to feel a bit better. For now, put your worries aside, comfort yourself and lay your head down on that soft pillow. That day is coming.

Who are you going to be with

Every moment of the day

Every day of the week

Every week of the year

Every year of your life?

Yourself

So, it makes sense to treat yourself well

Things to Give Yourself Today

A kind word,

A massive hug,

A silly giggle,

A big smile,

A small treat,

A well-deserved break.

EMBRACING YOUR DEFEATED HERO

---※---

Get up
Show up
Don't give up
Until eventually you rise up

---※---

When everything goes to pot, I turn to stories, books, films and fairy tales. They comfort me because I can see my experience in someone else's story. In every story, there is a hero; the protagonist we admire, who we want to win, who we want to be more like. And in every good story, there is always the 'defeated hero' phase. You know, that bit when the hero in the story gets knocked down, they 'fail'; they lose the boxing match, the karate competition or they get rejected at the school prom.

In tough times, I have caught myself pretending that I am that 'defeated hero' in the story of my life. **I feel their feelings and I feel their pain. Because they look and**

sound and feel like mine. Viewing a phase in my life in this way has helped me to process what has happened, to feel emotions, to persevere, to trust and once again believe that I, too, can overcome this crisis and become the hero of my own story.

Give your 'defeated hero' some air time

MAKE TIME TO REFLECT

It may feel uncomfortable to have narrower horizons than you would like for a time, but know that this is crucial to your 'character development'. You are building more resilience. Allowing yourself to 'go internal' before you can go external again means you will be able to deal with the next 'fight' much more easily when it comes. You will know your opponent's moves, their strategies; you will have recovered, you will have worked on your skill set and you will be ready. Ready for the next phase when the musical montage starts and you start training again. Every time you feel impatient or lose trust, remember there is a reason for this.

BE A HERO TO YOURSELF

Just like we want the underdog in a story to win, give yourself the same unconditional encouragement, love and support. Speak well to yourself and about yourself, and make it a habit. It can make a huge difference. **Be the one you believe in, the one whose story you know works out all right in the end. The one who is just facing a challenge right now but will pull through.**

FIND YOUR MENTOR

Defeated heroes always have a mentor - someone who tells them the truth, encourages them to believe in themselves and inspires them by their example. Who is that person in your life? If you don't have one, can you find one? Someone who doesn't sugar-coat things, but tells you the truth - what you need to hear not what you want to hear - and who believes that, with hard work and support, you will rise again and at the right time. Someone who tells you that no matter what has happened, you are already a hero to them.

RECONNECT WITH WHAT YOU STAND FOR

The 'defeated hero' always goes through a scene where they lose all faith in themselves, what they stand for and what they are fighting for, and they start to question everything that they were once so sure of. They might even be tempted to align themselves with their 'opponent' or question their life mission. You may also question or doubt all of these things and yourself too. Remind yourself of your values, what's important to you - this can help you cope with any kind of defeat. Your life is no mistake. You know yourself and what matters to you better than anyone. Don't let this one defeat you.

Your values inform who you are
And who you are informs your values
Don't lose either in the face of adversity
Instead, do the opposite and build
them even stronger

The defeated hero always rises again, so have no doubt that you will too. Just give this chapter, this scene, this bit of the soundtrack, the airtime that it deserves.

How Are You Really Doing?

› Stop and notice how you really are. You have to be honest with yourself before you can be honest with others.

› Tell someone who loves you. Reach out for their support. Never feel ashamed. We all need someone at some point.

› If you're having a rough day, don't beat yourself up about it. Just get through today, there is always tomorrow.

› Stop being a slave driver to yourself on the tough days. You need the opposite right now.

› You are your own hero. You need yourself in this moment, more than ever.

SWEEPING IT UNDER THE CARPET

Deceiving yourself is so much more painful
than lying to someone else

'You know what? I'm glad it happened. It wasn't really
right for me. It's a shame, but, honestly, I'm fine. I'm over
it. I've already moved on.'

Ever said these words but known with every bone in
your body that you did not believe a word that you were
saying and that the very opposite was true? That actually every part of you was hurting from something lost
that you loved? That every morning your heart hurt and
every evening tears rolled down your face? That every
moment of every day you felt totally crushed by life?

Sometimes we say things like this to protect ourselves
from those around us who we don't want to be vulnerable
in front of, and that's fine - we must choose our counsel
wisely. But when we say them to ourselves and to those

we do feel comfortable opening up to, that's when the problems start.

In the past, I would automatically revert straight to the 'moving on' phase without allowing myself time to process everything that had happened. When something ended or I experienced loss, I was fantastic at clearing out stuff, visiting charity shops with boxes, getting a haircut and tidying up my contact list on my phone. But that 'moving on' was only ever at a very superficial level. Don't get me wrong, these things can be helpful, but when they are done too speedily or without the emotional processing, or from a place of trying to feel in control, they never work. I thought that if I removed all physical reminders of the pain and of what had been lost, I could remove all the emotional pain too. But, of course, I couldn't and I didn't.

If we don't allow ourselves an emotional and mental 'spring clean' - which naturally takes time and work - we can end up in denial, find it difficult to express our emotions and feel impatient without knowing where this frustration is truly coming from. Crucially, we end up not learning the lessons that are being presented to us by life. Lessons that can serve us well in our growth.

Sweeping things under the carpet only takes you so far. One day, a tiny word, a small event, a song on the radio or bumping into someone who reminds you of what has happened or of your past life will rip that carpet up and expose all that pain and all those hurts that have been hidden. So, do yourself a favour. Don't sit in denial.

Sweep up, don't sweep under. Better still, hoover up, clear out that filter and empty out the hoover bag. We can't truly move on until we do the work. **Facing up to reality and seeing the situation for what it is, warts and all, is the only way that you will be able to move on.**

How do you avoid doing the denial thing?

FIND BALANCE

Our emotional systems need time to process feelings, slowly but surely healing that hurt. And we also need to have a break and distract ourselves when the processing of all these feelings gets a bit too much. Sometimes you will need to cry about it, talk about it or scream about it. And sometimes you will need to get away from it, have some space from it and not have anyone bring it up. We need to find that delicate balance of 'fake it until you make it' and 'feel it and be with it', and get comfortable with when we need each.

Balance Matters

> Don't forget the 'yin' in all that 'yang'. Make sure you are 'being' in all that 'doing'.

> 'Always busy' is not a badge of honour or your USP.

> Rushing, stressing and constant action is not balance. At some point you'll topple over.

> You are not a machine. You were not made to always work, to always produce, to always churn things out. If you need a reminder – you're human.

BE PATIENT

Your heart will take longer to heal than you want it to. Pushing and forcing things before they are ready to move forward just wastes energy. Trust it will happen. I am the worst person for being patient, but I have learned that my impatience is really the part of me that doesn't want to face difficult emotions or look at the hurt I am feeling. It took a long time for you to get into that crisis or life setback, and it will take a while to heal from it too. But be reassured it will happen. Ironically, often the more patient you are with the emotional processing phase, the more meaningfully and more quickly you can heal. You can't rush these things. So don't.

BE THOROUGH

A spring clean isn't just about dusting the surfaces - we move the furniture, open all the windows, rummage under the bed and rearrange our wardrobe. In the same way, we need to dig deep on our feelings and not just skirt around them. We can do this with the support of friends and family, of professionals, and with whatever it takes to help us heal mentally, emotionally and spiritually. **To welcome in the new, we must first address the old.**

RELEASE YOUR WORRIES

Talk about your worries, write about them, express them in whatever way you can. Start to learn about what kinds of strategies help you with worries and with your feelings. Is it mindfulness, is it a chat with a friend, is it problem-solving exercises, is it working out, is it volunteering to help others so you forget yourself for a while? Try out different tools for worries and see which ones best suit you.

BE OPEN AND AUTHENTIC WITH PEOPLE YOU TRUST

You will find the extraordinary thing about opening up is that you will make the most special and meaningful connections that you have ever known. Authenticity pays off and drops denial in the dirt. Surround yourself with friends who encourage you to be who you truly are and who don't allow you to sweep things under the carpet - the ones who look under it when they come over. A bit like food takes time to digest, being real with a trusted friend helps us work things through and move out of trying to push away how we feel.

Feeling heard is the first step to feeling understood. Can others hear you? Are you listening to yourself?

I need...	Please say...
To feel heard	'I will listen to you'
To feel supported	'I will help you to problem-solve'
To feel grounded	'I will reassure you'
To feel balance	'I will remind you to take a break and breathe'
To feel loved	'I will show you that you matter and that I am proud of you'

IDENTIFY THE LESSONS

Start to think about the lessons that life is offering you. Identifying these lessons can help you to really start cleaning stuff up and clearing things out, rather than ignoring them. What has been your part in what has happened? What was the other person's part in it? What factors outside your control contributed to it? What can you learn about yourself? Just as a scab forms a strong, protective barrier over a physical wound, so learning our lessons can heal our emotional systems and build resilience.

Denial never gets us anywhere. Facing up to the truth is hard and it's tiring. But pretending is harder and it's absolutely exhausting.

CHALLENGING FEELINGS

There's no 'should' or 'shouldn't'
to feeling emotions
Each has a place and a purpose

'If you're not on the list, you're not coming in.' But they are. All those emotions and feelings we are told not to feel – the ones we are taught are 'bad' from a young age and that we think we should push down at every opportunity – are all on the list. Not only that, they have VIP invites, automatically sent out to them after we've had a major life setback.

The real charmers are Anger, Shame, Despondency, Despair, Sadness, Guilt, Hurt, Abandonment, Frustration and Jealousy – a list of house guests that would make any party host turn out the lights, hide under the duvet and pretend they're not in when that doorbell rings. We had planned on the more popular crew of Happiness, Joy,

Hope, Connection, Positivity, Peace, Success and Excitement coming, but they are all at home washing their hair right now. Ironically, however, it is the most unwanted house guests who will actually make the party worth having. It will be totally wild, it will be extremely messy and it will definitely be different. But the party's worth having because it will teach us more about ourselves than we could ever imagine.

Challenging feelings can help you to:
ask for support
learn about yourself
understand those around you better
be loved and love

I was always labelled a 'sensitive' child and a 'worrier', and I grew up in agreement because worries and feelings were a big part of who I was. But, I remember the precise moment in my early twenties when I suddenly realised that I was not my feelings; that I felt them but I had the power not to be them. It was the biggest revelation for me and it was such a relief – and it was the beginning of me starting to embrace my feelings rather than push them away. And that is the real power that is in your hands right now, and you can use it. I promise. It is not something that other people do. It is something *you* can do too.

We can learn so much by just feeling our feelings. **Every feeling has a reason for being there and a purpose that it must fulfil:**

> Do you need to process something?

> Do you need to learn about who you really are and what your values are?

> Do you need to understand that your power lies within you, not outside of you?

> Do you need a reset and realignment of where you are going in life?

> Do you need to start valuing yourself more?

How to manage these house guests

LET THEM IN

Anxiety, fear, sadness... and all the rest. These are natural feelings that we all have. They are not nice to feel, but they are not going anywhere. When we accept them, they can move through us faster, with more ease, with understanding and with lessons learned. Feeling our feelings is a skill and, with practice, we can learn to invite them in and not be scared of them.

Your Emotional Toolkit

> Understanding. How do you react, what are your triggers, what do you need?

> Awareness. What are your thoughts, your feelings and how do you act?

> Strategies. What works for you – music, exercise, art, connection?

> Choice. Which tool works for which emotion?

> Practise. You'll start to trust that you know what to do.

ADDRESS THEM BY NAME

Naming the emotions we feel is helpful. It creates space between us and them in that moment. They then lose their mystery and their vagueness. We can sit down with them and find that place of power where we can really be with them, process them, manage them and feel them. It is in our power to choose strategies that can help us to allow our feelings to move through with more ease, more understanding, and so we can learn invaluable lessons from them. With time and by using these strategies, we start to feel better. Sit and notice what is going on in your body. Switch your thought of 'I am anxious' to 'right now I am feeling anxiety'. Naming your emotions means you don't have to be them.

LET THEM EXPRESS WHO THEY ARE

Let those uninvited feelings show you who they are - get your feelings out any which way you can: speak them, write them, dance them, draw them, bake them, garden them, run them, walk them... You can then see them more clearly, process them more easily and be less likely to be overwhelmed by them. **Self-expression is where your power lies when it comes to feelings. Don't let their energy build up inside you with nowhere to go. Give them a healthy outlet.**

HAVE A 'CHAT' WITH THEM

Your feelings are part of who you are. Chat to them at that 'party' and find out more about them and why they wanted to come. How often do they each need a chat or some attention or airtime? Understanding your feelings means understanding how you tick, how you work and finding more love for yourself. And this is where your power lies.

Just how in life it is sometimes those acquaintances you were least looking forward to meeting who become your best friends, the very feelings we don't want to feel can end up being our greatest teachers. They are part of your story too. **You don't have to pretend or put up a front. And that's a huge relief. That's precious.**

Ways to Manage Challenging Feelings

> Anxiety: breathe, ground yourself, talk to someone who cares, reassure yourself.

> Sadness: cry, get support, take comfort in kindness, listen to music.

> Powerlessness: problem-solve, set goals, stick to a routine.

> Anger: pause, run, drum, sing, move, write.

> Bad temper: create something to look forward to, have a sleep.

> Despondency: go out in nature, spend time with animals, look for good news stories.

> Jealousy: accentuate your individuality, write down three things you are grateful for and are proud of, say well done to others.

DEALING WITH BLAME, OUR INNER CRITIC AND FAILURE

It can sometimes feel like 'what's the point?'
But remember YOU are the point
You matter
Never give up on yourself
You deserve so much more – and be reassured,
it's on its way

After things fall apart, we might come across a few surreptitious and sneaky traps laid out, waiting to catch us in their snare and stop us in our tracks.

BLAME

One classic trap is blame; to blame anything and everyone possible - ourselves, others, life. We are really comfortable with blame because it helps us feel a sense of control. If we believe someone or something is to blame, or indeed that we are, then we can convince ourselves that, if we change ourselves, or them, or it, we will be safe in future from similar hurts. So we blame to give ourselves a false sense of security and protection from pain. But all blame does is just keep us in the past.

Our brains understandably try to make the mess - the unfairness and the unpredictability of life - into something tangible and logical. We airbrush the story, ourselves and others. We take away the imperfections; we distort reality and morph our memories of what happened into a story that feels more acceptable to us. **But simplifying what has happened just so we feel more in control does not help us move forward.** It doesn't do justice to what has happened or to how we feel.

Blame never helps. Shame never helps. They just keep you stuck.

Taking responsibility for your part helps. Understanding how your behaviour was not in line with your values helps. Both parties taking responsibility for what has happened helps. Being fair and kind to yourself helps. All these things help you to move forward. They help you to create your future.

Stop Airbrushing

> See the futility and wasted energy in blame.

> Remember there are always two or more sides to every story. Can you see all of them?

> Talk it through with someone you trust - get their honest reflections, not just what you want to hear to justify your original position.

> Be honest. What do you need to take responsibility for?

> Take action to put it right. Write a letter or send a text, apologise and make amends.

> Ask others calmly and respectfully to take responsibility for their part and you do the same.

YOUR INNER CRITIC

Have you got a loud, harsh and unrelenting inner critic? I have. For a long time, I didn't even recognise they were there. I tried pushing them away, silencing them or distracting myself from them. But they only got louder. A better alternative is to notice them, accept they are there and politely tell them that you are not going to listen anymore. And then counterbalance them by creating your new inner best friend – your best supporter and your greatest encourager. Practise creating your daily thoughts, words and actions to be consistently kind and gentle. It is a habit that we can all create given time, practice and patience. It's a habit that can change your life.

How to Be Your Own Best Friend

> Recognise and give yourself what you need in each moment.

> Say well done to yourself often – and really mean it.

> Realise you are more than enough. Not for what you do, or for what you 'achieve', but for who you are.

> Be gentle because life can be hard.

> Be kind to yourself – it's not selfish, it's essential.

FEELINGS OF FAILURE

Another trap we can fall into is our tendency to feel like we have failed. It is easy for us to feel like a failure when we are slap bang in the middle of a situation, but take a step back. If someone else was telling you this as their story how would you view it? Failure is inherently a judgement and you are in charge of how you judge something. Getting some perspective is powerful.

Feeling like a failure is a total waste of energy and time. See failure for what it is - a story bound by comparison and written with judgement:

> Comparison of where we are now to the 'standards' we have set ourselves of what we 'should' be doing, what 'should' have happened and who we 'should' be.

> Comparison of our lives to others around us and not feeling 'good enough'.

> Comparison of ourselves, our situation and our lives to society's expectations.

Just like track and field athletes stay in their lane, stay in yours. Focus on your life and your journey. Comparison is the thing that springs the trap of feeling like a failure. It is an unhealthy habit that can be broken and transformed into a healthier one. Realise that the 'standards' and 'stories' you are comparing yourself to are yours to make, not anyone else's and certainly not the shiny version of how your life 'should' be - these are all lies that you have been sold. Don't believe them anymore. **Why on earth do you want to be anyone else but you? You are amazing.**

Avoiding the Comparison Trap

> Notice when the word 'should' pops up in your words or thoughts. Change it to 'could'.

> Be aware of feelings of jealousy or envy. Don't judge, just notice.

> Reduce time on social media or work networking websites when you are having a tough day.

> Realise comparing yourself to others is futile. You are you. They are them.

> Don't waste your energy on comparison. Instead put it into being the best you can be.

FEAR OF LETTING GO

When I was a student, I crazily agreed to a tandem skydive. I couldn't sleep the night before, I couldn't eat breakfast, I couldn't keep my knees from shaking as I put on the equipment. I was utterly terrified. As I kneeled

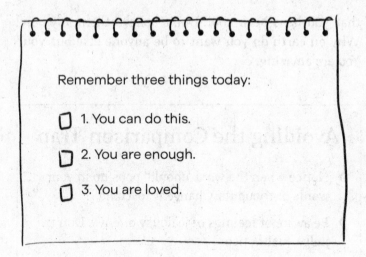

Remember three things today:

☐ 1. You can do this.

☐ 2. You are enough.

☐ 3. You are loved.

shakily at the open plane door, the fear was making me sweat. It was horrible. It was too late now. There was nothing I could do. So, I jumped. Freefalling was amazing. No more having to worry: I wasn't the one in control, I didn't have to be responsible for anything, it wasn't all down to me. It was a moment of utter relief. And I laughed. What had happened to the fear? I was more frightened up in the plane with no immediate threat to my life than I was in that moment when I was hurtling towards the ground. That didn't make any sense at the time, but it does now. Whatever happened, I had had to let go of control. And that was amazing.

How to Let Go

> Recognise when control is futile. It just wastes energy that you could put towards another strategy that will actually help you.

> Notice what happens when you try to control things – it is often the opposite of what you are trying to do. It restricts, suffocates and eventually sucks the life out of your dreams. It ends up pushing away the very thing that you are desperately trying to hold on to.

> Reimagine your dreams and what they could look like. Whatever has fallen apart wasn't working in that form. Trust that, eventually, when you get through this, life will bring you what is meant for you. Let go of the old dreams so these new ones can be found.

> Don't diminish your power by falling into the trap of being frightened of letting go. It's natural to feel frightened, but do it all the same.

The same is true of life. Although when things fall apart it can be the worst thing ever, if you look a little deeper often there is also massive relief. You are finally unshackled after such a long time spent trying to restrain, control, mould and shape things into the way you think they should be. When you let go, you are granted freedom from trying to 'keep things together'. Often it's the 'trying to keep things together' phase that is more stressful than 'the things falling apart' bit. **Letting go and surrendering to what is happening is really freeing. And, when you feel free, so many good things in life can happen. That is where your power lies - in letting go.**

In challenging times, we often uncover and discover many things about ourselves that we never knew before or didn't want to see. Some we are proud of. Some we may want to change or drop. It is all good. It's all useful information if we use it well. **Know that, even if you do fall into one or several of these traps, you can be rid of them and free yourself for good.**

REFRAMING REST

Let your shoulders fall
Let your jaw relax
Let your eyes close
Let your mind be quiet
And let yourself rest

After a major setback in life you need to rest. But all too often we just carry on being busy or try to get busier so we don't have to face what has happened. We might recognise that we need to slow down, but don't give ourselves permission to actually do so. We might feel that we don't 'deserve' to rest. Combine all these with the fact that we live in a world that pushes productivity and outcomes with relentless aggression, even when it comes to socialising and hobbies, and we are heading for trouble. **We have to consciously give ourselves permission to have a proper rest after things fall apart.**

The first step in doing this is to recognise that it's not an achievement to push yourself to the point of burnout.

It is not a badge of honour to *always* be *so* busy, especially in the midst of or after a really tough time.

I remember moving home several times in a very short space of time. Every move I had took another bit of mental, emotional and physical energy. When I got settled after my final move I started to make all kinds of plans for the other areas of my life. A good friend of mine reminded me that I needed to just stop and rest for a while. Part of me was trying to catch up on what I thought had been 'lost time' and I suppose part of me was trying to make myself feel that my life was still in an 'acceptable' state. Acceptable for whom? I was fine, but I was making other people's opinions more important than my own.

Step back and see the bigger picture. What's actually happened? What are the consequences if you don't stop and take some rest? And what exactly does 'resting' look like to you?

Reframe rest and what it can do for you

SLEEP

It would be easy to think that sleep is just lying down and not doing anything for eight hours. If that was the case, then it wouldn't be my first priority if my whole life was falling down around me either. But it's not. Sleep is an active process: your body repairs itself, it processes what has happened through the day, it lays down memories and it's crucial for us to be able to cope mentally and emotionally with tomorrow's challenges. And it's not just about quantity, but quality. Sleep is a necessity, not a luxury. So treat it as such. Make sleep a priority.

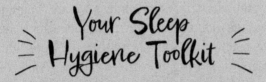

Your Sleep Hygiene Toolkit

Develop a routine that helps your brain know it's bedtime soon:

> Keep bedtime and wake times regular.

> Make your bedroom your sanctuary of rest.

> Get deep pillows and cosy blankets.

> Diffuse some essential oils, put on soft lighting and play some calming music.

> Avoid anything scary before bed – turn off the news, avoid horror films, don't read emails and don't think about the meaning of life.

> Write down three things you are grateful for. You'll sleep well.

JUST DO NOTHING

Sometimes having a rest means just doing nothing. And that is classically what you might think of when I say the word 'rest'. We all need time to just stop and stare, have a blank mind and watch mindless TV. Don't listen to the internal judgement telling you that you are 'wasting time' or 'being lazy'. It's an old message that society tells us still - that unless we are 'being productive' we are not of any worth, that we have no value. I had a teacher who would tell us we were 'idle' if we were caught staring out the window. Don't listen to that voice anymore. Sometimes, though, rest also looks like activity. Having a rest from life means getting away from all the bits that are stressful or feel like they drain you of your vital energy. Rest this part of your brain and conserve your mental energy by getting involved in activities that make you feel alive. Knitting, painting, singing, rowing, cycling, crafting, digging, baking - anything that makes you more in the present moment, right here, right now.

SCHEDULE IN REST

Yes, it's simple and it's boring but you need to do it. Otherwise, all that life admin will just take over like an aggressive weed in a flowerbed, squeezing out and suffocating any opportunity for the beautiful flowers to emerge. When you schedule something, you are giving yourself the message that it matters and then, in time, it becomes a routine and something that is normal and part of life, not purely a treat or a one-off. How often, when, where and what does rest look like in your diary?

REST WITH A CAPITAL 'R'

Big life setbacks or many small ones use up large amounts of mental and emotional energy. You are already likely to be in a state of 'rest deficit'. So, you need big rest. Be gentle and kind to yourself, and rest a lot and often. If you don't do it now, it will catch up with you and you will have to do it later, and maybe for much longer. Don't ignore your needs.

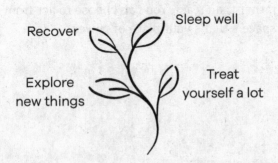

Recover

Sleep well

Explore
new things

Treat
yourself a lot

Rest is an essential item not a luxury one.

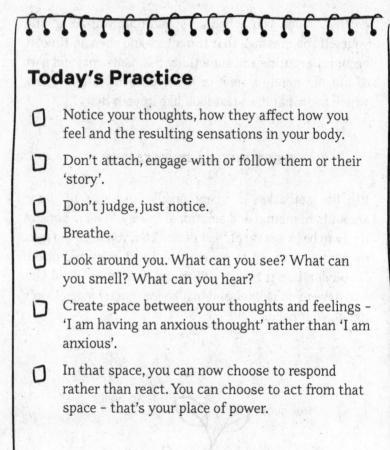

Today's Practice

- ☐ Notice your thoughts, how they affect how you feel and the resulting sensations in your body.

- ☐ Don't attach, engage with or follow them or their 'story'.

- ☐ Don't judge, just notice.

- ☐ Breathe.

- ☐ Look around you. What can you see? What can you smell? What can you hear?

- ☐ Create space between your thoughts and feelings – 'I am having an anxious thought' rather than 'I am anxious'.

- ☐ In that space, you can now choose to respond rather than react. You can choose to act from that space – that's your place of power.

KINDNESS AND ALL THOSE HURT PLACES

If you do something today
If you speak something today
If you think something today
Make sure it's with love

Life hurts sometimes. We all get hurt and we all hurt other people.

We can't avoid hurt, but we can heal it. **There's one thing guaranteed to heal all those hurt places, and that's love. And kindness is love in action.** Just like when we get hurt physically and we clean, dress and treat our wounds to help them heal, so kindness is the balm to our emotional wounds.

How many times have you heard people say, 'You just need to be kind to yourself' or 'Just love yourself'? We would all like to love ourselves more, but what does that look like? And how can we do it?

I used to be the worst person for not being kind to myself, and occasionally I slip back into my old ways. One moment that will stick in my head forever was when a friend of mine said to me, 'Radha, I wish you were as kind to yourself as you are to everyone else.' That made me cry, but in a good way. I finally realised just how unfair I had been to myself and, to be honest, I just felt really sad for myself. Why had I been so unkind to myself and about myself for so long? There was no good reason that I could find for it - just a bunch of ideas and beliefs that I had absorbed or interpreted incorrectly.

When things go wrong in life and we blame ourselves or feel like a failure, it's even harder for us to tap into our kinder selves, to find the energy and willingness to love ourselves. But it is precisely at these times and exactly in these moments that we need to do this even more than usual. Kindness is a choice, and even if we don't find it an easy one to make, we can still try to make it. Without even realising it, we have been making the choice to be unkind to ourselves, so now, knowing what we know, we can choose to be kind towards ourselves instead. And you'll be relieved to know that **it's not huge, one-off gestures that really make the difference; it is often the smaller, less obvious and easier to achieve actions that count.**

How can you be kind to yourself?

GIVE YOURSELF WHAT YOU NEED

If your baby cries, you give them a cuddle; if your dog is hungry, you give them some food; if your houseplant is looking dry, you water it. You are no different. It sounds obvious, but the next time you feel unloved, just notice what it is that you are not giving to yourself. Is it a kind word or thought, is it an early night, is it saying no to an invite, is it texting your friend to say you need a chat? You deserve your own attention, respect and care. **You deserve to have your needs met.** Don't continue ignoring your own needs, and don't keep compromising them for others either. Get familiar with your needs and fulfil them.

PRAISE YOURSELF

We don't say well done to ourselves enough. These two short words have extraordinary power and can have a huge impact on how we feel. A simple 'well done' gives us the positive reinforcement that we need to carry on. Praise presents a sneaky trap though, because we can get it confused with validation. Society tells us that we are of 'value' if we earn lots of money, if we are in a relationship, if we pass lots of exams, if we are busy all the time, if we own a home. Don't listen. Instead, make sure you are praising yourself for who you are - a kind, wonderful human being - not what you 'have'. Praise is a cornerstone of our self-esteem and mental health. **Make praise a habit and sprinkle admiration all over your daily affirmations.**

Give yourself a good
soak of kindness

If you feel
unloved, devalued
or unheard

A dry, thirsty plant soaks
up every last drop of
water it is given

SPEAK KINDLY ABOUT YOURSELF

Words matter - they have huge power. If you say something about yourself enough times, you will start to believe it. Notice the thoughts and words that you think and say about yourself. How many of them are unkind, harsh, critical and unforgiving? Even if you find it challenging to jump straight from those to kind ones, think about how you can rephrase thoughts and words so they are 'less unkind'. **Gradually, with practice, you can move up the scale from unkindness towards kindness.**

BELIEVE...

...in yourself, in your life and in your future. That is kind-ness. **You have a choice every day in what you choose to believe and what you choose not to believe.** Think of the people who love you - one thing they all have in common is that they believe in you. Follow their example and love yourself. Think about all the things you have coped with, managed and got through. If you keep forgetting and lose faith in yourself, write a list of them and look at it every morning. Don't fool yourself into thinking you have to be better before you believe in yourself. You'll be better for believing in yourself right now. And you deserve to.

BE PROUD OF YOURSELF

Don't just be proud of what you do when things are easy and circumstances are in your favour. Think about all the times when people around you weren't supportive, when you had to dig deep all on your own, when it felt like everything was against you. And how you carried on, what you achieved and who you showed yourself to be. That is really something to be proud of. Be proud of your-self for making 'mistakes' and learning from them, for getting it wrong and trying to make it right, for giving up and then getting up and carrying on. Don't skirt around, skate over or negate your achievements, and only focus on what you need to 'improve'. Celebrate yourself: treat yourself to a meal out, a shopping trip, a small break away, a bunch of flowers or a new bit of tech.

DON'T ACCEPT ANYTHING LESS

Reject unkindness from others. Tell others when their words or behaviour are not OK. Say no to people when they demand things of you. Every time you reject or challenge an act of unkindness and lack of respect towards yourself, you show yourself that you matter. These are all acts of self-kindness. Establishing your boundaries with others can help you firm up your boundaries with yourself.

The more you are able to practise self-kindness, the more you are able to heal from all the hurt. **Kindness is a gentle wave that washes over the hurt and smooths out the ripples of sadness in the sand.**

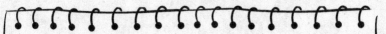

Things to Be Proud Of

☐ Getting up and out of bed today.

☐ Letting someone know you are struggling.

☐ Your willingness to be vulnerable and opening up.

☐ Being gentle and patient with yourself.

☐ Making choices in each moment to help yourself feel better.

☐ Looking for the kindness and the good in spite of it all.

☐ Your wisdom in knowing things needed to change.

☐ Spreading love and hope for yourself and others.

☐ Your courage in stepping up.

☐ You, no matter what.

Kindness is not a concept

It's a way of living

Kindness is not a soft skill

It's a life-saving skill

Be kind to yourself

Who told you that you deserve
anything less?

THE POWER OF GRATITUDE

Turn 'Here we go again'
Into 'I'm grateful to be here again'

When we are in deep, everything is dark, monotonous and heavy. All we want is to feel good just for a tiny moment, just for a bit, to give ourselves a mental break and a bit of relief. We wait to feel good, thinking that it will happen if something would just change, if we could just get something or if things went back to how they were. And we wait and we wait and we wait... That's the danger - we could be waiting forever. And forever is a long time to wait to feel better.

A sure-fire way to feel a bit better is to use gratitude as a daily tool. It works - money-back guarantee level. It can take you from the depths of despair to feeling better in a moment. **And you don't need to look far to find things to be grateful for. They are already all around you.**

Your gratitude toolkit

START SMALL

Are you grateful for your bed, a place to rest your head? Are you grateful for something to eat? Are you grateful just to have got through the day? Are you grateful for a drama-free work meeting? **Don't reserve gratitude only for the big or the grand.**

MAKE GRATITUDE A HABIT

By making gratitude a habit, we automatically start to notice things to be grateful for in real time, we notice them faster and we notice more of them. To help it become a habit, try saying thank you for something every time you wake up in the morning, every time you brush your teeth or every night when you go to bed. Try creating your own gratitude book and write in it every day. Whatever works for you, stick to it, and do it often. Notice that, when you do, you feel better, and your brain will do the rest and make it more of a habit. Eat, sleep, be grateful and repeat.

BE GRATEFUL FOR OTHERS

Look around you. You will find people who are your champions, who support you, who are always there for you; buying you small treats, cheering you up, texting you back late in the evening to check how you are. Say thank you and show them that they are appreciated. It will make you feel better to recognise you have people on your side and it will make them feel good too.

Every single one of us has the power to inspire
positive change in our world

Through our voice, our actions and just
by being who we are

Never forget the power you have

Never forget to use it

BE GRATEFUL FOR THE LESS OBVIOUS

Be grateful for the 'bad' stuff, the tough stuff, the less obvious stuff. It is often the difficult times – the crises – that help us learn our most important lessons and to become more of who we really are. Being grateful for the tough stuff is radical and can have radical effects. Start saying thank you on those days when everything seems to be going wrong. It helps us give up judgement of what 'should' happen in life and frees us from expectations. That's real progress.

If you want to get somewhere that feels just a tiny bit better, then get there faster and more easily by being grateful.

A Grey Day

> A grey day doesn't have to mean a 'grey feeling' – you can always turn it around.

> Sprinkle colour through your day with happy thoughts and a rainbow of gratitude.

> Wear your brightest clothes, socks and underwear. It can make a big difference.

> Embrace the grey. Get cosy, get comfortable, get snug.

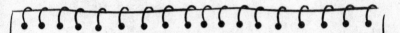

Things to Be Grateful For

- [ ] Having someone who cares about you.
- [ ] Your strength and how you have coped.
- [ ] The birds that sing, the wind that blows, the sun that rises.
- [ ] Having something to eat and somewhere to sleep.
- [ ] Having this moment.
- [ ] Yesterday. No matter what happened. What did you learn?
- [ ] The people you love. The kindness of strangers.
- [ ] Your health.
- [ ] You and who you are becoming.
- [ ] Your unique purpose - the reason you are here on this planet right now.

PUTTING YOURSELF FIRST

You need to realise
That all you need right now
Is to have your own needs met

I can already hear that inner voice in your head judging the title of this chapter and here is my response: no, it is not selfish; it is absolutely necessary. You have been through a lot. Your reserves are low. You are exhausted. You are running on empty. You need space and time to reconnect with yourself. You only have so much capacity to help others. If you ignore the need to put yourself first, you could end up tipping into overwhelm and emotional burnout.

Reconnecting with your needs first may have become a totally foreign concept to you. You may have spent many years putting others before you - your partner, your children, your friends, your wider family or your work;

in fact, everything and everyone possible. It's become a habit. We might be told that this is an admirable thing to do or be guilt-tripped into it because that is what a 'good' person does. It's not either of these things and it's not something to be proud of. Of course, all of us have responsibilities to care for the people in our lives. And yes, it's great to look after others, but not at your mental and emotional expense. Ignoring your own needs may have contributed to this crisis situation in the first place, so if you want to look after others, look after yourself first.

How to put yourself first

RECLAIM YOUR NEEDS

Ignoring our needs is something that is drummed into some of us with an unremitting relentlessness throughout our life. We are told that we must be a 'good person' and a 'good person' should compromise their time and should always put others first, and shouldn't voice their needs. **But all these 'good people' end up losing themselves in the process.**

Don't believe it anymore. It's untrue and it's damaging. Why don't you deserve to have your needs met? Why do you put yourself in second place, further down the list or last in line? Who told you that you should do this? What have been the repercussions of doing this in your life so far? What would be different if you put your own needs on a level with or sometimes above others' and how different would you feel?

SCHEDULE IN TIME FOR YOU

It's diary time. You need to actively commit to spending time on yourself, no matter how busy you are. Look ahead, plan and write it down in black and white. Communicate clearly with the people in your personal life and at work about how things are going to change. Don't let anyone or anything get in the way. Yes, take their ideas into consideration, but don't let them sway you back into old patterns. As well as longer-term scheduling, you need to develop moment-to-moment strategies too.

In each moment think: How can I put myself first in this moment? Is it a bath, an early night? Is it to say no to someone? Is it to say yes? Is it to go out for a cycle? What or who is stopping you? And why are you giving away your power to them? **By scheduling in time for you, you are signalling to others and yourself that you deserve your needs being met too.**

RECONNECT WITH PEOPLE WHO ENCOURAGE IT

Maybe you have lost touch with the people who know you best while you have been busy with life. Perhaps reconnect with those who knew you from a time when you did put yourself first. Maybe they are old gym buddies before you left your gym, or from your coffee morning group that you just got 'too busy' to meet up with every Saturday morning. They can help you remember why you deserve to do this again. Don't feel ashamed to reach out or feel uncomfortable because you haven't spoken for a while. They are the ones who can help you remember why all those things you used to do or that time you used to set aside for yourself needs to be reclaimed.

DISCONNECT WITH PEOPLE WHO DRAIN YOU

You may need to disconnect with those people who are not good for you in your quest to put yourself first. You know... the ones who ask lots of personal, intrusive and information-gathering questions. The ones whose real agenda or intentions you are unsure of. The ones who enjoy gossip. The ones who, after you tell them what has happened, come straight back with all the things that are going well in their lives. The ones who just make you feel worse - down, tired and used. Putting yourself first means stepping away from these people.

Nurturing Healthy Relationships

> Respect yourself.

> Feel free to say no.

> Be consistent.

> Don't compromise who you are for someone else's approval.

> Drop fears of judgement and negative reaction from others.

> Act with integrity.

> Be authentic.

BEWARE GUILT MANIPULATORS

These are people who put their agenda first. They believe their needs are more important than yours, that they should always come first and that you should toe the line. And, if you don't, they will pull out all the stops to make you feel guilty and responsible for their upset and like you are a 'bad person'. I will let you into a secret - you will never be able to make them happy. And it is not your responsibility to either. **We are all responsible for our own happiness.** Even if you give up your entire life and all your needs, it will never be enough for them. Knowing this frees you from trying. Recognise these guilt manipulators, try to explain things to them, but if nothing changes, create space away from them.

By not putting yourself first you are making yourself small. **You deserve to take up space in this world, so allow yourself to be seen.** Value yourself and put yourself first.

Things You Can Do to Put Yourself First

☐ Run a bath and take a long book with you.

☐ Call an old friend and have a proper chat for a change.

☐ Put 30 minutes of 'me time' in the diary each week – and don't delete or cancel any of it. Keep that promise.

☐ Turn off notifications on your phone for half an hour so you can get away from it all.

☐ Put aside some money to buy yourself a treat every so often.

☐ Forget what other people want to do. Just do something fun for yourself for a change.

WRAPPING COMFORT AROUND YOU

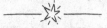

Keep going
The only way is forward
While you wait to feel a bit better
Comfort is the 'better' that you can
find right now

To feel comforted is no small thing. We don't talk about it much, but we should. Being able to self-soothe is everything. When we feel safe and secure, physically and emotionally, we make better decisions, we are more likely to be able to start our recovery process and we can begin to feel a bit better after a setback. **Taking a comfort break should not just be a euphemism.**

Think of comfort as anything that gives you the same feeling as a huge, warm, soft blanket that you wrap around you when you feel vulnerable. It can help lessen fear, anxiety, sadness and despair. Think of it as a protective shield that is yours to pick up when you need it. It is worth spending some time thinking about what comfort looks like for you because it can really help in tough times.

FEAR versus LOVE

Fear drains you	Love sustains you
Fear can overwhelm you	Love can be overwhelming
Fear has its place, but needs to be kept in its place	Love is who we are, its place is inside all of us

So, choose LOVE for yourself and for others

We often grow up looking for other people to comfort us, and it can provide a way to connect. But, when we are solely or totally reliant on others doing this for us, we feel vulnerable when they aren't around to do it or just can't, and we put a lot of pressure on our relationships. Eventually they crack because no relationship can withstand that amount of reliance on it. When we are able to comfort ourselves in balance with others comforting us, we can start to trust ourselves. We know that no matter what happens, where we are or who is around, we can help ourselves feel safe. We have that power inside us and we will never be without it.

Set about designing a 'comfort kit' for those raw days, when the world feels harsh and unfriendly, and when you just want to hide. That kit can go with you always and you never have to be without it. You just have to be aware of what's in it and when you need to use it. Just like how you would pack the things you need for a weekend away and unpack them when you got there, pack what you need for those tough days and unpack your comfort kit in each tough moment.

Ask Yourself...

> How can I feel safe and secure right now?

> What can reassure me in this moment?

> What's making me feel uncertain and ungrounded?

> How can I soothe myself?

> Do I know that even if I feel like I am alone, I'm not?

What might be in your comfort kit?

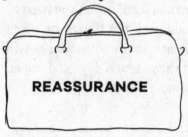

Deep belly breathing, feeling your feet on the ground, addressing your worries and reframing the worst-case scenarios into less scary ones can help you feel comforted. Speak to yourself as if you were a small child who is scared. Let them know that, even if they feel frightened, you are here for them. Let them know everything will be OK.

A soft jumper, a pair of slippers, an old pair of jogging bottoms, a nice scent of perfume, a warm bath, hot chocolate, getting into bed... All these can help us feel relaxed and remind us of calmer times.

THE BASICS

Not being hungry, cold or tired is a good start to feeling comforted. When our basic physiological needs are met then we are more likely to be able to feel calm and safe. Beware hunger and tiredness when life setbacks are in full force - avoid them at all costs, especially 'Hangry', which can be the most vicious of opponents. They are the basics. Don't forget them in all the turmoil.

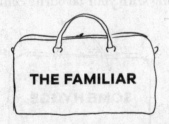

THE FAMILIAR

This might be the nostalgia of an old audiobook, a classic TV series or something that lifts you up or reminds you of happier times. These things can help you feel safe in situations that may be changing rapidly. Old friends who have known you your whole life are precious.

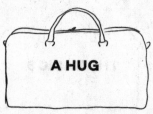

A HUG

A hug from yourself, from others, with your pet, a teddy bear or a soft cushion always helps us feel comforted. However old we are, our bodies will always respond to hugs through the release of feel-good chemicals into our systems. **Hugs come in many different forms: give your feet a hug with some warm, soft, fluffy socks; give your hands a hug with some nice-smelling moisturiser; give your mind a hug with your favourite comedy show.**

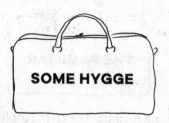

SOME HYGGE

'Hygge' is the Danish concept of cosiness and content-ment. Light a candle, make your home feel inviting, enjoy the simple pleasures and surround yourself with pictures, flowers, colours and textures that make you feel comforted. Make your home like a children's nursery - have a reading corner, a quiet corner and a cosy corner. They will all give you different types of comfort when you need it most.

Feeling Comforted Is...

> A song that reminds you of happier, calmer times.

> Candlelight, a bath, a good sleep.

> A cup of tea and a biscuit.

> A smile, another person's voice.

> A squeeze of a hand, a gentle touch, a soothing hand on your forehead.

> A word of encouragement, a generous thought.

> Knowing that today is over.

> Realising you've done all you can.

When we get familiar with knowing how to comfort ourselves, we get more and more confident in our ability to do it. That confidence and self-reliance to find comfort is where your power lies. **Make your comfort kit an essential luggage item. Carry it with you wherever you go.**

Some Days...

> You don't need to 'do'. You just need to 'be'.

> You need to cry.

> You just need to go back to bed.

> You need to let go of any expectations of yourself.

> You need to just wait until tomorrow.

'WHAT NOW?'

Learn from the past, but don't let it define you
Open your eyes to the future, but don't look too
far ahead
Focus on today; it is where real change, real
opportunity and real joy reside

When crisis hits, we hold our head in our hands and say, 'Now what? Not another thing.' But with time and some healing, we eventually start to ask 'What now?' instead and that's a really good sign. 'What now?' hints at a sense of acceptance that we are where we are. It's a sign that perhaps we have given up past expectations, resistance and trying to control. And that is a major step forward in our journey. It's a nod to the future, which is amazing, but it can still feel hard, knowing that something needs to change, but still being really unclear about what on earth that means.

How to embrace the next step

DON'T LOOK TOO FAR AHEAD

Take things day by day, hour by hour, moment by moment. This avoids mental and emotional overwhelm and means we can deal with the day-to-day issues and practicalities of life that are still running in the background to the best of our ability. One step at a time, one breath at a time. Slowly, slowly you will realise you can take a bit more on.

Make Things Micro

> Readjust your mental timeline to the next moment, the next hour, the next day. Forget the next month or year for now.

> Break down big problems into smaller bits, and tackle them one by one.

> Remember your well-being is the sum of lots of small daily actions, not a few grand plans.

> Create small things to look forward to.

> Notice small acts of kindness and accept them wholeheartedly.

DON'T EXPECT TO KNOW

It's times like these when you need to give up all expectations of knowing how anything is going to turn out. Own the 'not knowing'. When we think we know everything, we are asking for trouble because life usually has a very different plan for us than the one we have for ourselves. **When we own up to not knowing, anything is possible.**

STAY HOPEFUL

It is hard when you can't see a way forward, but remind yourself of times gone by when things did work out, when everything was OK in the end and how you coped in those times, even though you had no clue about what would happen. Hope helps us remain open to the idea that things can get better. Ask others to remind you of what you can be hopeful for right now.

BEWARE YOUR BRAIN

Your brain is the biggest cinema projector of worry that could ever exist and creates the worst-case scenarios when it doesn't know for sure what is going to happen. Don't blame it – it thinks it's doing what it can to try to protect you and keep you safe. Try to get time away from your brain – with hobbies, meditation, exercise and seeing friends. There is a difference between thinking and problem-solving. Thinking for the sake of thinking only causes worry and anxiety. Problem-solving is specific, focused and outcome-based. So focus more on problem-solving.

RECOGNISE WHAT YOU KNOW

You know that something needs to change. That's a huge step forward. To have learned that for now is more than enough. As the 'Now what?'s reduce in frequency and intensity, so the answer to 'What now?' will be slowly revealed. Until then, just hold on and keep going.

'What now?' holds positivity within it – a hint of forward movement. You are ready and willing to move to the next step on your journey, up and out of what has been, into what could be.

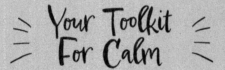

> Ground: Feel your feet on the ground.

> Breathe: Deep belly breath in, hold, out.

> Visualise: Close your eyes and go to your 'happy place'.

> Relax: Lie down, clench each muscle group in turn and release.

> Love: Imagine sending love and receiving it from others.

> Treat: Flowers, hot chocolate, fish and chips.

STEP 2

Stepping Up

Don't ask...
Where I have been?
What have I done?
Who was I then?
Instead, ask...
Where am I going?
What will I do?
Who am I now?

You feel like the rawness of the loss, the disaster, the crisis has softened slightly. You feel like you can feel your feet on the ground just a bit more, you can breathe more easily, you can sleep a little more soundly.

You've got through. Well done. That's huge. And in the process, you've found something inside you that has an energy all of its own. Something has been set loose. You've discovered that power you have inside yourself to get through anything and survive.

But it doesn't stop there. Stopping now would be like trying to hold back a wave about to crash or a volcano about to erupt. It's not possible. Now, it's about stepping up to try to dig deeper; to understand the past and what brought this crisis to your door, and why. By doing all of this, you will learn more about who you truly are. This is where your power lies.

It's going to take courage, patience and a lot of hard work. You are going to have to be honest with yourself and stay the course. But I promise you, it will be worth it. It's in the stepping up to the challenges you now face that you are going to discover just how powerful you are and how you can work towards changing things up too. And change is where this story ends.

But, for now, roll up your sleeves and take a deep breath. It's time to step up. I know you can do this.

Your Power

› Step up, step forward.

› It takes every ounce of courage, it takes all your willingness, it takes real heart.

› But know that it's the best step you could ever take.

› Your power is unearthed in that step.

› Take it because you deserve it.

› And because it has been calling to you for so long.

LOOKING FORWARD

A shift will always happen in the end
But that 'end' is actually just the
start of another one

There isn't always a well-defined moment when we realise that we have switched up from getting through the aftermath of a crisis to being ready to step up and accept the challenge of facing the 'What now?'.

This forward movement happens subtly, without us even realising it consciously. Then one day there will be a moment when we suddenly realise that things don't feel quite so heavy. There is a little more space around our feelings and we can see a bit more clearly. We are being a little kinder to ourselves and there is some hope when we think about the future.

But, let's be clear, the 'What now?' challenge is only an invitation. You can choose to accept it or not. If you do, then change is on the horizon. If you don't, then it may be that the time is not yet right for you. It can take many setbacks and life crises for us to wake up, see clearly and learn lessons. And that's OK. Don't judge yourself. The invitation will arrive in your inbox again and again and, when the time is right for you, you'll accept it.

Let's take a relationship breakdown as an example. It's over, you've got through it, you've had some rest, you've licked your wounds, and now you feel like you can be out there in the world a bit more. And you could just leave it there. But, if you do, you might find that, in time, the same issues, problems or patterns recur in your next relationship, and you're back to square one. But, if you step up to the challenge to try to understand and unpick what happened and why, and what needs to change and how, then you have an opportunity to really heal, to break the cycle and to thrive in your future relationships.

Any change requires action – a realisation, a decision and a willingness to look at what has happened – not just intention or belief. And that is what stepping up is all about.

Step up to the challenge because...

YOU MATTER

Whatever has happened and whatever you think about yourself right now, I want you to know that you matter. You deserve to give yourself a chance.

YOU'LL LEARN VALUABLE LESSONS FOR LIFE

Lessons need to be learned and learned well. Ignoring them is only going to give you repeat experiences in the future. Commit to being open to learning and wanting to learn. You may need to learn lessons more than once, so don't be surprised or disheartened by that. Although some lessons might be hard, you'll never find a better or more useful teacher.

If you keep your eyes, ears and heart open you can always learn something new
From every single thing that happens to you
From every single person you meet
From every feeling you feel
From every challenge that comes your way
From every opportunity you are offered

THINGS CAN BE DIFFERENT

Your past informs your present and your future, but it does not have to dictate it. Things can be different for you. Believe and trust this is true. That alone can carry you a long way.

IT'S A COURAGEOUS THING TO DO

Accepting the invitation to go through the challenge requires an active decision on your part to want things to be different. Doing something different is scary. It is easier for us to stay in our old, comfortable ways of being, even if they are not helpful to us. But for things to be different, you have to commit to making them so.

IT WILL BE WORTH IT

Stepping up to the challenge is not going to be easy. It will take hard work and it will take time. It may even feel worse for a while. You are going to have to dig deep, unpick what has happened and feel some challenging feelings. But, in the end, know that nothing worthwhile comes without effort. All that effort will pay off in the long run.

Don't be fooled - stepping up to the challenge doesn't just happen. It's an active decision. And, right now, it is yours to make.

FACING UP
TO THE PAST

It is useful to visit and learn from the past
But not to live there forever in ignorance

Things happen for a reason. I believe we can learn something from every experience we have. Sometimes the most worthwhile lessons are the ones that are the toughest to go through. The past is powerful. It is useful in understanding what, how and why something has happened, but the limit of its power should stay there. **Your power lies in what you do now, in the present.**

Just like the way sometimes your computer will flash up a message saying it shut down because of a 'problem', things often fall apart in our lives because something wasn't working. There was a problem. Now you have a choice: do you want to carry on as usual, running the same old programs and apps as before, potentially creating the same problems again, or do you want to run a piece of software that can detect what caused the issue, 'fix' it, learn from it and 'restart'?

If you embark on scanning the software that has been running your life so far, you'll find some bugs and glitches, and will need to frequently scan files again to make sure they haven't come back. In a similar way, when we face up to the past it can bring up a whole host of ghostly characters and obstacles that can get in your way. Although your first reaction is to run away from them, in actual fact you need to meet them and face them down, once and for all.

What might turn up in your Haunted House of the Past?

GHOULS

Self-doubt, shame, denial, resentment and other such ghoulish characters will rear their ugly heads while you are trying to understand the past. They will pop up at times when you thought they were properly back in their box. They may make you want to sound the alarm and evacuate the haunted house, but you have to take courage and keep going. Listen to them, see them for what they are, and understand why they are there and what you can learn from them.

THE REGRET TRAPDOOR

When you start to see the past for what it is, you start to see what could have been done differently. And you can fall into the regret trapdoor. You will know you are in it if you are using a lot of 'should's. 'Should' is rigid and unforgiving. Try replacing it with 'could'. 'Could' is a proactive word and creates possibilities for your future.

You may be 'wishing' a lot too; wishing that things were different or you had done things differently. You may also spend a lot of time in the past, in conversation, in opportunities and in your routines. Beware, this trapdoor only faces downwards and it takes a lot of strength to climb out again. It will keep you stuck in the past and no good comes from lingering there.

THE TIME MACHINE

The past has extraordinary momentum. A small event, thought, word or song can drag you right back into the past. Your brain replays images, memories, showreels and highlights of the worst bits. Realise you can step out of this momentum. Get active, use your body, change your environment or create a distraction if the momentum is too strong. Or talk about it, reach out for support and sit with it if you have the energy to do so in that moment. A balance of the two works well. Staying in the present moment with mindfulness, breathing techniques, taking notice of what's around you and slowing down can all help.

Grounding Yourself

> Feel every inch of the soles of your feet connecting with the floor.

> Focus on each of your senses. What can you see, hear, smell, feel and taste?

> Use your breath. Deep, slow. In, hold, out. Repeat.

> Say to yourself, 'I am OK and I am safe.'

> Put on a song, go for a run, look at the clouds, touch a tree, feel some earth.

Leaving the past behind is a choice. Although it's a tough one to make, it is where your power lies and the only way you can move forward.

You forgot you had a choice

You forgot that you have power

You're remembering to choose
differently now

You're remembering that you are
actually that power

DROPPING YOUR SECURITY BLANKET

Hold on to the things that help you
Let go of the things that don't
Deep down you already know the difference

In times of challenge and hardship, our well-established and set behaviours provide us with a security blanket. Some of these behaviours may still be helpful, but some may have contributed to the problems we find ourselves facing, are still contributing to them in the present and will contribute to their reccurrence in the future. If we hang on to these just because they help us feel 'safe', we can't move forward, we don't 'grow up', we can't stand on our own two feet and we will never be free of the past. These behaviours give us a false sense of safety. They are in actual fact doing the opposite of keeping us safe.

Maybe you turn down new job opportunities because you are frightened of failing; maybe if your friends let you down just once in a tiny way then that friendship is over; maybe you start earning well but end up spending too much so your bank balance is always a struggle to keep in the black; maybe you abandon your needs over and over again because you feel guilty if you put yourself first. These are all patterns of behaviour that exist because once they gave you a sense of safety and security, and they served a purpose. But now they don't. They are to your detriment instead.

It's hard to throw off certain behaviours, even if these patterns are harmful to us. We still want to cling on to them like a security blanket – anything rather than stepping into new and unfamiliar ways of being. **But just because something is comfortable, it doesn't mean it is good for you.** The time comes in every child's life when they must throw their security blanket away, and you must do the same. It can feel scary, disorientating and like you are on shaky ground for a while, but in the long run, it is necessary. **Hold on to the things that help you feel comforted *and* that serve you. Drop the things that are giving you a false sense of security and that harm you.**

Throw off your security blanket by...

RECOGNISING PATTERNS

Talk it through with a friend, write about it, watch films that resonate and read books that you feel drawn to. All of these can help you understand past triggers, patterns and behaviours. Were there any recurring themes? A lot of patterns come from a place of not feeling good enough and from low self-esteem. What can you work on in yourself that will help you to drop these behaviours and not repeat these themes? Ask for support if you need help doing this.

CHANGING YOUR RESPONSE TO TRIGGERS

You have a choice about whether you react or respond. Reactions tend to be instant, emotional and entrenched in the old. They are so automatic, we sometimes don't even realise until afterwards. Can you identify these triggers, take a breath and allow space between them and your reaction? Can you choose to come from a more considered, calm and centred place and respond instead? Practise.

FINDING COURAGE

Be brave. With any hard thing that you have to do, think about the repercussions of not doing it. Remember, the old patterns kept you stuck and caused you unhappiness. You don't want that now and you deserve more. Remind yourself every single day in those tough moments that you are brave, and make a commitment to keep trying, however hard it might be and however long it takes. Doing hard things takes courage. I find it helpful to consider how hard things might continue to be if I don't make a change.

BEING PATIENT

One day, you'll understand fully why you needed your 'security blanket', and you will also realise that you don't need it anymore. You'll be able to say 'thank you, but no thank you' to it. You'll see that you can do all the things you wanted to do without it. You'll prefer your freedom to being trapped in the illusion that these behaviours keep you 'safe'. But it will take time, so be patient with yourself.

It's a bit like that moment when you take the stabilisers off your bike and manage to stay upright and moving forwards without them. You realise you don't need them anymore. **With that freedom there is no limit to how far you might go.**

Finding Certainty in Uncertain Times

> What can you control? Focus on that. That is where your power lies.

> Create structure in your week. It will help ground you.

> Be certain in the moment-to-moment choices you make for yourself.

> Get practical. What are your options, what are your safety nets, what is available?

> Remember there is certainty in love and kindness so invest your time in these.

> Be confident – you're a safe bet.

REDISCOVERING JOY

Happiness begins with you
Joy lives within you
They aren't something outside of you
They are you

When things have turned upside down, it is natural to focus on the hard stuff, to 'tackle' things, to get to the bottom of it all and to have tunnel vision in a relentless bid to find all the answers. To feel the anxiety, the stress and the worry. But what about the joy?

It's at the very time when we find it hardest to find joy that we actually need to focus on it, create it and cultivate it even more. Because it will be the one tool we can use consistently and reliably to help us get through.

Joy Is...

> You being yourself.

> The simple and small.

> Free.

> Found in revisiting what you loved doing when you were little.

> An expression of love for yourself.

> All around.

Joy is not just a word in a fairy tale or a warm concept; it's a daily tool that helps us feel better. It refills our emotional energy. It reminds us that, even though right now things are tough, every moment does not have to feel tough. When we share in something joyful with someone else we don't feel quite so alone. It brings us hope. Think of it as the water stop in a marathon race - you can't miss it; you need it to keep on going.

For me, joy is very different from happiness. Joy comes from inside. It's a sense of contentment and it can be present despite challenge. Happiness tends to be short-lived, affected by outside events, and is much more susceptible to disappearing in tough times. Happiness is like a bright, hot, intense summer's day, whereas joy is a warm, inviting glow in a window on a cold night.

How can you feel joy in the midst of challenge?

SCHEDULE IT IN

Life is so busy that we actually have to schedule in joy. It sounds strange, and I know scheduling sounds anything but joyful, but it works. Every day set aside 30 minutes to do something that brings you joy; something that fills you up and gives you a feeling of contentment and connection.

REDISCOVER YOUR JOY

We are born to feel joy and we found it easy when we were little. Whatever brought you joy back then can give you a clue about what you can do now, as an adult, to find joy again. Was it painting, messing about in the garden, pretending you were presenting a TV cookery programme in the kitchen, singing into your hairbrush or dancing like no one was watching? It was for me. Whatever it was for you, try it or something like it again.

BE SPONTANEOUS

Feeling sunshine on your face, listening to a bumblebee in the park, laughing with a friend, taking a warm bath with a good book or the feeling of putting on a pair of fluffy socks... spontaneous moments of joy feel even better than the scheduled ones. There are plenty of opportunities for these spontaneous moments every single day, if you stop, slow down, allow them time to arise and notice them. **Forget outcomes; focus on just being in the here and now, and you'll experience more joy.**

RELEASE YOUR INNER CHILD AND
YOUR INNER ANIMAL

We take too much notice of what we are told we 'should' do, how we 'need' to behave and what being an 'adult' means. In my view, mostly these things are really serious, dull, templated and boring. So boring. Children and animals don't need to work at being joyful and they certainly do not hide their joy. Children sing, dance, laugh and express their joy. Dogs wag their tails and cats purr whenever they want to. Reject the idea that you 'have to behave' in a serious, 'adult-like' way. Be more like children and animals, and, if you can, spend time around them. They will remind you of how joy comes naturally and is easy to find when you don't listen to all you are told.

LET THE MUSIC PLAY

Play music that makes your heart sing as well as your voice. Rewrite that love song, where the lyrics were written about someone else, with you as the subject instead. Offering yourself kindness and love will help you to find more joy. Music is a guaranteed way to find joy so listen to as much as you can.

FILL YOUR HOME WITH JOY

Create your own joy meter. When you look at that picture hanging on the wall, what level of joy does it bring you? How about the feeling of your feet on the carpet as you get out of bed? What about the smell of fresh flowers or perfume in your room? Fill your home, your handbag and your car full of things that work with your five senses to bring you more joy. Make each environment where you spend time score highly. And make that joy yours.

Joy is the very thing that can fill up your emotional reserves and help you through challenge. Don't put it in the corner - put it centre stage. If you choose one thing today, choose joy.

JUST IMAGINE

Allow yourself to dream
Allow yourself to imagine
Allow yourself to create your future

All too often, we use our imagination to scare ourselves, to generate the worst possible scenario. But we can also use our imagination for the better - to imagine what we want, what our lives could look like and how things could be. We get to choose how we use our imaginations. So why not use them to help us feel better?

I love using my imagination and get frustrated whenever I go to places where the creative activities are only for children. I want to have a go; I want to use my imagination too. I've realised that when I use my imagination I am doing so much more than just 'daydreaming'.

Your imagination is a powerful tool. You can use it every single day in so many different ways and all with the same outcome if you use it wisely - to dream, to visualise, to create your future and, ultimately, to help you feel better. Don't ignore it, don't tell it that it is childish and should be quiet. Use it. If you haven't played with your imagination for a while, that's OK. Get back into reading books, create something of your own, listen to music, paint, draw, colour, decorate, listen to stories... Anything creative will help you get back in touch with your imagination.

Imagining helps by...

TAKING US AWAY FROM REALITY

Our imaginations can take us into a whole new world, into a new emotional state. We can have a mental break from the stresses and strains of life. Visualise your happy place, use your senses to imagine what you might see, hear, smell, taste and feel. Give yourself a lovely, free five-minute holiday away anywhere, anytime. We can transport ourselves to new worlds, to new places and, importantly, to new feelings.

UNLOCKING FUTURE POSSIBILITIES

To imagine is to dream. And to dream is to create a vision of the future possibilities for your life. Imagination is not based on anything our senses are experiencing right now, but on things that have not yet happened, but that could.

Take a few moments every day to sit and imagine the kind of future you would like to create. What would it look like? How would you feel? What might be different? Paint your life. Write your story. There is no limit to your imagination.

Have a Virtual 'Mini-Break'

> Book it. Realise you deserve and need a break. Schedule in time to relax.

> Prepare for it. Turn off your phone. Forget the washing. Forget life admin.

> Pack your bags. Where's your happiest, most calm and peaceful place?

> Travel there. Use your imagination to take you there. Visualise and sense it. What can you see, what can you hear, how do you feel?

> Enjoy your trip. Empty your mind of all the worries, of all the stress, of everything. You don't have to purchase a return ticket if you don't want to.

ALLOWING US TO SEE OUR TRUE SELF

Forget you are you for just a minute. Imagine you are your favourite book character, someone you respect in your family, someone you admire. Imagine you have all their strengths and skills. And imagine for just a moment that you are them – this is especially useful in those moments of self-doubt, demotivation or self-sabotage. 'Be them' just for a little while. You'll soon start to realise that the attributes and skills you admire most you already have. You can uncover your unrealised actuality and untapped potential.

PUTTING US IN TOUCH WITH OUR INTUITION

When you get offered a new job or you want to move to a new area, how do you know if it will be right for you? You have some facts and some knowledge which helps, but what about using your imagination to help too? What would your new routine be like? What would it feel like to wake up in your new home? 'Going there' can help you decide if it's the right choice to make. Your imagination can also help your mind be more flexible, to solve problems and think up new and previously unseen ways of overcoming obstacles.

GIVING US HOPE

When we are at our lowest, it is hard to see how our present reality could ever transform into something better. We can imagine that tomorrow things might just be a little bit better, that next year they could look completely different. Our imaginations can help us see that something else could be possible and can help us find hope again, even in the darkest of times.

Extraordinary inventions, incredibly moving art, life-changing technology and so much more have come from one person just sitting down and imagining. **Extraordinary things can happen in your life when you awaken your imagination.**

Make the word 'next' your daily mantra:

> Next moment.

> Next choice.

> Next thing.

> Next step.

And just take one 'next' at a time.

FEELING ANGRY

If you push anger down over and over again
It will eventually end up pushing
you down instead

Feelings exist on a spectrum - we can slide up and down, left and right, along this scale in how we feel from moment to moment.

When you step up to try to understand the past and what has brought things crashing down around you, you can feel a lot of feelings. You go through the whole range. Sadness, anxiety and fear are feelings we are often told we are 'allowed' to tell people about. But what about those feelings that are not spoken about very much? What about feelings of frustration, irritability and anger? Unfortunately, society has often encouraged these to be covered in shame and we are told to hush them up. If we are a 'good person' we 'should never feel angry'. Nonsense. **We need to feel all of our feelings and shouldn't feel ashamed of any of them.** They all have a purpose. In fact, in human history things have been changed for the better because people felt frustrated and angry at something that they recognised wasn't just or fair. All feelings have a place and a purpose, not just a select few. And if we don't address them, they will cause us even more distress in the future.

You might feel frustrated and angry at life, at yourself, at others, or just angry at everything. Maybe you feel disillusioned or betrayed or abandoned. Anger is a powerful emotion and can help us rise to the challenge. There is energy behind every emotion; a momentum and impetus underneath that, once we understand, we can harness in a healthy way to help us move forward into change. **Frustration comes served with an aperitif of challenge, a bouquet of action and subtle undertones of change.**

When I feel angry, what I have noticed is that underneath a lot of that anger is actually fear or sadness, a feeling of not being seen or heard or something that I am looking for that is not being given freely. I also know that it has been feelings of frustration and anger that have helped me to make changes in my life and in the world. They have motivated me to make something better. When I get angry at something, I want to work to change it. And that can be helpful.

Just like we move our fingers up and down on a keyboard to hear the next note on the musical scale, so moving through feelings like anger and frustration can help us to move forward, transforming sadness or fear

139

into change. But in order to do this we need to learn how to express and process our anger and frustration in a healthy and safe way.

Managing feelings of frustration and anger

Have some time away from others.

Accept and recognise they're there.

Visualise breathing frustration out and calm in.

Allow yourself to feel them.

Sing, run, drum and dance them out. Write down how you feel, use a journal. Talk about it.

Recognise that another feeling or a need that is not being met often underlies these feelings.

Watch or listen to something calming.

Ask yourself or others for support to have that unmet need fulfilled.

Work on strategies of how to turn frustration into motivation towards healthy change.

Act to process them in a healthy way so they can move through.

How can you move through and past anger?

FIND WHAT'S UNDERNEATH IT

Sadness or powerlessness often underpin anger – sadness that one of your needs has not been met; powerlessness that you feel you cannot change something. Cry, express that sadness and get the tears and words out. You have lost a dream, a person in your life, a goal, or you may have lost yourself. Get it all out. It is only by processing the sadness or powerlessness first that you can move into a different energy and find your power.

DON'T FEEL ASHAMED

Feeling angry or frustrated doesn't make you a 'bad' person, it makes you human. Realise that anger needs to be felt and processed in a healthy way. You can use your body to get that energy out. Get out in the garden and dig hard, run as fast as you can, cycle like you are in a hurry, sing in your car like you mean it, go into a quiet forest and scream or shout. Your body wants to help express it all. Get support if you need help with how to express these feelings in a healthy and safe way.

LISTEN TO ITS MESSAGE

Every emotion has something it is trying to tell you. Anger is no different, and one of its messages is that you are feeling some kind of emotional pain, that you want something to be different, that you don't feel heard or valued. If you hear the message, it can give you a clue about what you need to give yourself or what you can ask others for support with. Why is the anger coming up? What situations trigger it? What helps you feel less angry? This is all precious information. If you need support to help you understand the message, ask for it.

DON'T MUDDY IT WITH BLAME

Anger can get tightly linked to blaming others for what has happened. Take responsibility for your part in what has happened in the past, and how things have turned out. Remember fault and responsibility are different. Owning your stuff from the past is your path out of feeling trapped and towards emotional freedom. It may feel temporarily better to blame others, to blame life and to blame everything including yourself, but **it will just keep you stuck in powerlessness, pain and unhappiness.** It will stop you moving on. See things for what they are, who did what and why, then let it go.

GET MOTIVATED

Use the disappointment, disillusionment, frustration or anger to make something change. Feeling angry can help you to get clearer about what you don't want and, in doing so, what you do want. What do you need to change? What do you want to take action on? Get stubborn, get determined, get moving. Get motivated.

Every emotion has its own purpose. Find its reason for being there. And work on healing that.

FINDING YOUR WHY

To be authentic, you have to act with integrity
To act with integrity, you must live your values
To live your values, you have to know what they are

There have been times in my life when things have not gone my way, when obstacles have reared their heads - from not getting that work project I wanted, to taking on more responsibility caring for family or having to end friendships or relationships that I thought would be there forever. These obstacles have varied in nature and extent, but there's been **one universal consistent element that has always brought me out the other side: my 'why'.**

Life will always have its peaks and troughs - there will always be some minor or major crisis - but, if you can pinpoint your 'why', you will be able to manage whatever comes your way. The what and the how are easy once you know your why. So, right now, make why your starting point.

Your why is your purpose, but reframing purpose as your 'why' is a much more tangible, relatable and

Your Why

> You are here for a reason. Find it.

> Your power lies in your ability to choose how you respond. Use it.

> You are not defined by others or by your past. Drop it.

> You get to decide what your why is right now. Do it.

> Knowing your why will help you get through this and come out the other side. Trust it.

practical way to think about it. To me, the word 'purpose' conjures up visions of a grand moment of enlightenment while meditating, being involved in global humanitarian work or being the first person to go into space – something huge. I think a lot of us feel that, unless we know our 'purpose' right now, we are lost; as if we are missing something or 'incomplete' until we find it. Our 'purpose' can often feel like an inaccessible, mysterious thing that we will never find.

You can find your 'why' in those small moments where your heart is full, where you experience real satisfaction like this was everything you were meant to do and be. It can be anything from smiling at everyone you meet on your daily walk and helping them feel good, to getting totally immersed in painting a picture or doing your job wholeheartedly. What do you want people to say about you at your funeral? How do you want to be remembered? This might sound a bit morbid, but these answers will help you find your purpose. All of these things might give you a clue as to your why.

Don't stress about finding your why. Just notice what makes you feel alive and do more of it. Before you know it, you'll have found it. **Your why holds a huge amount of power when you are trying to step up to challenges. In fact, it *is* your power.**

Your why helps you to...

FIND YOUR TRUE NORTH

A bit like a compass when you are lost, **your why can help you to reorientate and clarify where you are going when you have been taken off course.** There is a lot of noise out there - other people's opinions, judgements, life events, so many 'should's - and these can get in the way of you following your purpose. Remembering why you want things to be different, why these things matter to you and why you don't want to settle cuts through all this noise so you can find your true direction again.

BREAK THROUGH THE NEGATIVITY

Just like a tiny fragment of sunlight peeking through the dark clouds on a rainy day reminds you the sun is still there, so **your reason for being here in this world can break through all the disillusionment, cynicism and feelings of defeat.** It can break through even the strongest of negativity. Let that crack of sunlight in.

PERSEVERE THROUGH DISAPPOINTMENT AND DELAYS

Knowing your reason for doing something helps you to keep going when things are hard and they aren't going the way you had hoped. **If you feel it is something worthwhile, it doesn't matter how long it takes.** You'll keep on going, even if it is not important to anyone else or valued by others - you know it's everything to you. Everything that is in your heart and you are passionate about. You realise that you can't abandon it because that would mean abandoning yourself. And then you will be totally lost.

BE MORE 'YOU'

Your 'why' is a reflection of who you are. Like your reflection in a mirror or in a crystal clear river, you see yourself in it. Finding it helps you to celebrate your individuality, and gives you more freedom to be yourself, to find your voice and to express your incredible skills and talents. And this feels really good. You will start to grow in confidence and step out of that tendency we all have to conform. **You won't want to be like everyone else; instead you'll want to be more you.** That's true power.

Express Yourself...

> To feel heard, valued and loved.

> To build self-esteem and confidence.

> To show the world how unique you are and to be proud of that.

> To truly connect with others.

> To have fun, to bring joy and for the world to benefit from you being you.

The best investment you can make is to stop, reflect and get clear on your why. It changes your life. It gives you something you can trust in, something to hold on to and something that will never leave you, no matter what.

Your purpose in life is not dependent on anyone else's recognition of it

It is dependent solely on you owning it

GIVE UP GIVING UP ON YOURSELF

Remember today's 'bad day'
will be tomorrow's yesterday

You may think that you haven't given up on yourself. But, pause for just a minute and look back at what has happened in the past. If you are being honest with yourself, you may realise that actually you have. We all have at some point. You may catch yourself in the mirror with tears running down your face, or being stood up again by someone, or compromising your time for a boss who decides to land an urgent email in your inbox late on a Friday. **We have to see that we deserve more than this and we have compromised too much. And realise that if we don't change something, we will lose ourselves even more.**

There are certain moments in life when you realise that enough is enough. That you have lost yourself.

But also, that you matter. That you deserve better. That you have been compromising your health, your well-being and your happiness for too long, in too many ways and without any return, whether that's been in a job, a relationship, a family dynamic, a friendship or a set of circumstances. It's OK - that's in the past. The question now is: are you going to realise that you have also been giving up on yourself for far too long? Are you going to do something about it? Are you going to take this opportunity to make a decision? Decide no more, no longer, not again. Decide that, instead, you are going to give up giving up on yourself.

Choose to persevere against all the odds to change things up in your life so that your true worth and value are reflected back to you. To do this you have to understand why you might have given up on yourself in the first place.

There are many reasons why...

OTHERS

Other people we interact with in life can make us feel that we are not enough: what we are told about ourselves when we are growing up, behaviours that we have allowed others to get away with or the world at large valuing things that we don't appear to possess. **Believing others' opinions of us over our own is a dangerous thing. Don't**

make anyone else's opinion about your self-worth more important than your own. You are the most robust authority on yourself and your life.

Fitting In...

> Is a step too far if you have to change who you are.

> Squashes your uniqueness, creativity and authenticity.

> Is something we are all told to do.

> Is different from meaningfully connecting with others.

> Doesn't make for an interesting life or world.

US

Our sense of self-worth often comes from society's 'should's; that we *should* have married by a certain age, that we *should* earn a certain amount of money, that we *should* own a property, that we *should* have children, that we *should* always be happy, that we *should* be there for everyone else except ourselves. Even writing this many 'should's exhausts me, let alone trying to live them out.

And the tragedy is that these 'should's are utter lies. **When we believe them and we haven't 'achieved' them, we make ourselves 'less than' everyone else.** We give up on ourselves.

Good Self-Esteem...

> Is simply what you choose to think and believe about yourself.

> Comes from not comparing yourself to others.

> Is in your power to change.

> Is a habit you can practise and build.

> Starts with small, practical steps that you can take right now.

> Can change your life.

LIFE

Life happens and difficult things happen. To help us makes sense of what has happened, we can interpret these things as our fault, that they have happened because we are not worth it or that we are destined to always experience 'bad things' because we don't deserve anything better. **Don't take it personally. Don't let what happens in life dictate your self-worth.** Things have more opportunity to change if you don't incorrectly interpret what has happened to be because you are not good enough. You are. It's just that life happens, that's all.

If you answer these questions honestly, after some careful consideration, you might find your answers don't actually make any sense at all.

Ask yourself these questions:

- ☐ Why do you think you do not deserve all the wonderful things that you dream of?

- ☐ What do you think you have you done that makes you so undeserving?

- ☐ Why are you giving up on yourself?

HABIT

If you find yourself slipping into that old habit of giving up on yourself, then let others remind you of how amazing you are. Call a friend and let them tell you all the reasons why they love you. Write down a couple of things that you are proud of yourself for. Recognise the beauty in you being uniquely you. Remember all the times you have stepped up for family or friends and supported them in their decisions, and reminded them to never give up on their dreams. Do the same for yourself now. See through the comparison trap on social media and turn it off, take a break from it.

You can give up on a lot of things, but never, ever give up on yourself. You are too precious for that.

Things you need to say a lot more to yourself:

> 'You are doing really well.'

> 'Keep going.'

> 'It will pass.'

> 'I am proud of you.'

> 'I'll look after you.'

REWRITING
YOUR STORY

Happiness begins by understanding who you are
It continues by creating habits that
match who you are
And it lasts by making choices that
reflect who you are

We all love a good story – it's how we can try to understand the things that have happened to us, connect with others and relate to life itself. We are born storytellers. Stories have incredible power and momentum; the stories we tell ourselves about our lives and the stories that other people tell about us and that we believe have far-reaching consequences. With every word you say about yourself and what has happened to you, you write another sentence in your story. Words have power. The story we choose to tell about our lives and how we frame that story ends up dictating our present actions and our future choices. What story do you want to write about what has happened in your life so far?

Stories...

> Transport you into other worlds.

> Help you to work through your feelings and process the ups and downs of life.

> Make you feel less alone, that you have a friend for life.

> Help you understand more about yourself and others.

> Have extraordinary power, so be careful about the one you write for yourself.

We all have a story of 'us': who we are, what we are good at, what we are not, how we will react in certain situations, what we do and don't like. And we all have a 'story' of how our lives have been, how our lives are and how they will be in the future. We believe this story like it's gospel, like it's ours, like we wrote the outline, the plot, the beginning and the ending. And yet usually we have had nothing to do with it. We get 'airdropped' into our story. We are expected to quickly adapt and be faithful to the script we have been given and play the role of the character we have been assigned, being true to their list of traits, their backstory and accepting of their future storylines. We all go along with this story for a while, because we don't even realise it is happening, until one day we start to question what that story is all about: who wrote it, how we got involved in it when we didn't audition for it and whether we want to be part of it any longer.

Maybe you were told from an early age that you are 'lazy', that you lack common sense, that you are always late, that you're a 'troublemaker' or that you are the responsible one who should always make the peace in tricky situations or conflict. Hearing this story often enough, you start to listen to it. And you start to believe it. This is when our involvement in someone else's story of us starts. Our beliefs change our perspective and perception of situations and dictate how we act. So, we 'become' our story; it's a self-fulfilling prophecy. We then don't need anyone else to carry on writing it. We ourselves take up the lead author role and strengthen the story by buying into it. We add our own paragraphs that only strengthen the narrative.

But what if you could step back, review the story, realise its inaccuracies and rewrite it? What if you could write your truth? Well, you can. **The first step is to realise that who you think you are may not be who you really are.** Seeing this truth can help you to change your approach to many different life situations.

How to Unravel Your Story

> Talk to people who know you from different areas of your life who may have seen different sides of your character.

> Look back at your past decisions. Do they really demonstrate what you have been told about yourself?

> Write a list of words other people use to describe you. Write a list of how you describe yourself. Do they match?

> Visualise the traits and characteristics in people you admire or feel lacking in. Think of times when you have demonstrated these.

This is not an easy process. It means being open to seeing yourself in a totally new way and in a new light. It's new territory and the unfamiliar is naturally scary.

You will feel a range of emotions when you 'rewrite' the story of you...

CONFUSION

When we start to unpick our story and see that we have been living in a way that is inauthentic it can make us feel really confused, question everything and push back. We can feel angry that we have believed everything we were told and have made decisions based on this. That's OK. Remember, your power lies in the present moment and you can change your story. No regrets; you have learned something, now move forward.

DISORIENTATION

You might feel ungrounded because everything you thought you knew about yourself has been turned upside down, so you might try to cling on to your old character role for a while. Even though it doesn't reflect who you are, you at least feel 'safe' there. That's OK - it took time for this story to be written, so it will take time to rewrite it too.

SELF-DOUBT

We have all been conditioned to behave in a certain way to gain approval and validation and to 'fit in'. But who has made these 'rules' and are they serving us or not? If not, what do we want to drop and what do we want to change? Beliefs are strongly ingrained into our systems from a young age, like grooves in a record playing the same tune over and over again. When we start to break free of that story, we will have periods of self-doubt. These can originate from us or from others who are resisting us breaking free of the story. Remember they have also been part of this old 'story of you'. Remind yourself of why this is important to you and surround yourself with a tribe of supporters who encourage you and who can see you for who you really are.

INAUTHENTICITY

Once you have unravelled your existing story, you will be under a lot of pressure to rewrite it into a well-known rigid storyline – you know, like one in those typical action-packed templated 'blockbuster' films. But, in my experience, they have no charm, they feel wooden and they don't keep your interest for very long... How then can you make sure you stay true to your authentic story? When planning a night out, do you ask what everyone else will be wearing, rather than wearing what you like?

Do you still feel duty-bound to go clubbing rather than out to dinner just because you used to rave it up when you were in your late teens? Does everyone still expect you to be the one who cooks dinner every Christmas? Slowly start to reset and reform family traditions and friend meet-ups to reflect more of who you are. Take small steps in being the real you.

Writing Your Future

> Find out about the main character - you.

> Vision and dream their future - it's yours.

> Surround that character with friends who lift them up - they are there for you.

> Give them challenges - you will evolve.

If we don't like the way things have been, **we can start to define and determine our own storyline moving forward. We can make our own choices and, in doing so, we get to decide how our story ends.**

UNCOVERING YOUR 'WHAT'

What do you want?
What do you need to change
to get what you want?

'I just want to be happy', 'I want it all to work out more than anything', 'All I want is for everything to be OK' – recognise these words? I do. I have said them often enough with tears rolling down my face. Crying helped me let my feelings out and relieve some pressure, but those sentiments didn't get me any further towards clarifying things. But the word 'what' did.

'What' in grammatical terms is called a 'determiner word'. It decides something. And you do too when you think about your 'what'. You are clear on your why – why you want things to change, why you are here and why you want to try to make things different – but now it is about your what. What does your new life look like? What would be different and what would be the same? What do you do in that dream job? What elements does that loving and caring relationship have? What would feeling valued by your friends and family really mean to you? You get to determine and decide what exactly you are going to invest your energy in, and what your future is going to look like.

We all want to 'be happy', but, in practical terms, this statement is really not helpful at all. It's not realistic. It's general and vague. It's pressurised. Statements like this can get in the way of making practical and tangible changes in our lives. Yes, we can feel happy sometimes and things can work out mostly, but not always and not how we think they 'should'.

Get clear about exactly what you want and specifically what you need to change

GIVE IT TIME

We are clear on the fact that something needs to change, but what exactly that is can take longer to work out. Be patient. Don't be afraid to move slowly. That way the changes are more likely to be a success and to be meaningful. Don't rush just because you are impatient or scared. Time has a magical effect on the most confusing jumble of thoughts and feelings. Time helps them to settle, like water after it has been stirred up in a pond, only allowing the useful stuff to rise to the surface and for the situation to become clearer.

BREAK IT DOWN

Big things are harder to pin down and are less tangible, which makes us less likely to act on them. Think of a tree. The trunk is 'I want to be happy', the main branch is 'I would like better relationships', the side branch is 'I am going to create more time and space in my day to see my friends' and the end branch is 'I will make sure I see my family for dinner once a week'. This might sound obvious and simple, but it works, trust me.

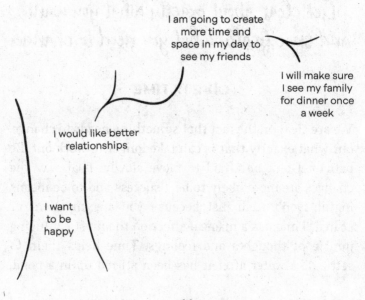

CHOOSE THREE AT A TIME

When we spread ourselves too thinly and try to do too much all at once, we will undoubtedly fall at the first hurdle. Only choose three 'whats' at any one time: three things you want to change. Go for one big priority that you find challenging and maybe two 'low-hanging fruit' priorities that are easier to achieve. For example, your three might be creating healthier boundaries between work and life, plus flossing your teeth and saying one thing you are grateful for every day. Once you feel you have achieved these things, create your next three.

MAKE SURE IT'S YOURS

We can absorb other people's 'what's. We take these on board as if they are our own, and give them undeserved attention, time and focus. Then when we achieve these, we wonder why we don't feel as good as we thought we would. That's because they were never ours in the first place. Ask yourself 'What do I want?' not 'What should I want?' Beware parental pressure, sibling rivalry, friendship comparison, relationship 'status' and job 'success'. These can all take us away from our own precise list of 'what's. There is no greater waste of mental, emotional and practical energy than chasing a what that was never yours. Hold your own ground and build firm boundaries around what *you* want to change.

BE FLEXIBLE

Life is dynamic and so are you. You are constantly evolving. Don't get stuck rigidly to your what if it becomes outdated; just because you have started doesn't mean you should finish. If you tell everyone about a career change, but you try it and it's not for you, that's OK - change your 'what' again. Don't get obsessed with an outcome or worry what others might think. It zaps your energy. Knowing what needs to change is a gradual filtering out process of what you don't like, and a gradual introduction of what you do. And we are filtering all the time.

When this is all over, do you want to truthfully say that you did your best? Or do you want a nagging, internal doubt in your mind that you could have done more? **Do your best, make the changes yours and you will thank yourself for it later.**

The Journal of You

> Create a journal full of what you know helps you.

> For each feeling you feel, write down what strategies help you feel better.

> Create an affirmation page – what thoughts and words inspire you?

> Create a gratitude page – what three things in your day are you thankful for?

> Create a page with names of friends – what support can they offer you and when might you need each and every one of them?

> Create a page of what you are proud of and why. Read it often.

NEEDING A TOP-UP

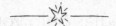

When things outside yourself feel unsure,
ungrounded and unkind
Trust yourself and go inside
Find that place that is sure, that is grounded and
that is kind
It's there and it wants to be found

Life gets so busy and, in all the hullabaloo, we forget ourselves - what we enjoy and what fills our energy levels up. We have got into a habit of putting ourselves last, we don't take the time or space to invest in ourselves and, eventually, we 'run dry'. Our habit of ignoring our own needs tends to get stronger and more difficult to break when we face setbacks in life. We just naturally fall back into old patterns. But it is now time for you to stop and remember: **Who were you before 'life' happened and what did you used to love?**

How did you get to the point where you had to ask yourself these questions? What happened? Maybe you have just broken up from a long-term relationship or got divorced after years of marriage; maybe you have just retired; maybe your children have moved away from home or your long-term caring role for someone else has ended. You have spent so many years and so much time investing in this part of your identity that you haven't invested in yourself, and that's understandable – we have all been there. When your identity changes, or that role is no longer there, you start to notice an emptiness – a gap – and that can feel really scary. You want to fill it up, but you don't know how or what to fill it with. You just don't know yourself anymore.

Realise that within that emptiness is space; space to get to know yourself again, to understand what makes you happy and to fill it with what you love and with everything 'you'. Life is calling you to remember and rediscover the parts of yourself you may have lost along the way, to top up and recharge.

How can you fill that gap?

RESPECT THE LOSS

When we lose a part of our identity or a role that we once had, we need to give that loss the respect it deserves. That means mourning it and giving ourselves time and space to grieve that loss so we can come to a place of acceptance. Unfortunately, we can't fast-forward or rush this. All we can do is be kind and gentle to ourselves and ask others around us to do the same. Love is where our power lies in these situations and can help you find yourself once more.

REMIND YOURSELF

Try to remember what you used to enjoy and what you used to do before the role of husband, wife, parent or employee came along. Think back to what you used to do with your time and rediscover it now. It can be scary to do this because it's almost like lifting the lid on an old box up in the loft. Will it make you happy still, will it make you emotional, will you be able to recognise and find parts of you that were lost for a while?

MAKE NEW CONNECTIONS

If you enjoyed a hobby once, find a local group, join a club, start that hobby up again, get out there and get involved. Not only will you potentially find a new role for yourself, but you will likely also find some new friends and connections. It all helps towards filling that gap that will progressively get smaller and smaller in your life.

It's not just about filling a gap from a lost role or a changed identity, but also about small steps you can take to refill your energy levels and find out more about yourself in the process.

What can you do to top yourself up?

GET OUTSIDE IN NATURE

The wind, the sun, the rain and the earth all hold a
magical power. They give us energy in every way possible.
They make us feel truly alive. The rawness, the beauty,
the peace and the perfect balance of nature has never let
me down and has always helped me feel restored.

MOVE YOUR BODY

Your body is a brilliant tool to help you recharge. Get
moving in any way you can - dance, run, jump, stretch.
You might think that you're too tired right now and
haven't got the energy to exercise, but, trust me, it's
the other way around. The more active you are the more
energy you will have.

REMEMBER TO LAUGH

Setbacks and challenges in life can understandably
make us feel heavy, cynical and serious. When was the
last time you really laughed, where your tummy hurt,

where you couldn't breathe, where you cried and it was almost painful because it was so funny? Probably not for a long time. Well, that needs to change. Laughter gives us energy. Stick on your favourite comedy show, watch stand-up online, be around animals and children. Surround yourself with as much joy and opportunity for a smile or for laughter as possible. Sometimes we self-sabotage when we feel under stress by watching the news, consuming more doom and gloom, getting involved in social media disputes and watching heavy, upsetting dramas. Make better choices for yourself. You can help yourself feel a tiny bit better.

Top up often, top up well and never let your glass run dry.

Smile Because...

> You deserve to.

> It will help you feel better.

> A little smile can give you a little break from it all.

> It recharges your depleted emotional battery.

> You can always find simple, small things to be grateful for, even in the worst of times.

> You are amazing and you are loved.

FINDING YOUR TRIBE

Sometimes in the darkness when we forgot we
could shine
We just need to find a tiny bit of light so we can
see our way again
Our friends are those precious little lights

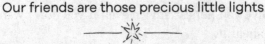

Ever noticed that you show different parts of you according to who you are around? You may feel like you shine in some groups, but are like a damp squib in others. Changing to fit in with our surroundings is necessary sometimes if we feel vulnerable, but if we do it too often we can find it hard to show our true colours.

One of the things to help you through challenge is to find your tribe of supporters - your 'family' outside of your family, your circle, your crew. Those people who lift you up, who inspire you, who support you and who understand you. The people you can really show your true colours to.

Best Friends...

> Can sing your favourite song.

> Can recount your most embarrassing moments.

> Laugh and cry with you.

> Lift you up higher than you thought you could ever go.

> Celebrate your successes and feel your pain.

> Stand up for you and with you.

> Give you honest advice even if you don't want to hear it.

> Are always there for you when you really need someone.

Friendships come and go as we change and grow. And the people who once understood us may not anymore. Even the family we grew up with may not 'get' us or just aren't able to support us in the way we need, even though they try. Find your group of cheerleaders who you really bond with. And, when you find them, really treasure them because making strong and meaningful connections with them is everything when you are finding things hard.

How to find your tribe

NOTICE

A good way to get clearer about who your tribe may be is to notice how you feel directly after you spend time with them. Do you feel exhausted, drained, full of self-doubt and wishing that you had stayed at home and washed your hair instead? If so, they are probably not for you. And how about the absent ones? The ones who only turn up for you when it suits them? Everyone has their own lives to lead, but you know the people who let you down all the time or when it really matters. Notice the ones who are supposed to stay in your life forever. They will be few in number, but they are worth more than you could ever imagine right now. They are so precious.

Never forget those who:

made sacrifices for you

lifted you up when you were down

kept you company when you felt alone

believed in you when you couldn't

loved you when you found it hard to

LET GO

We don't have to let go of relationships that are no longer for us with animosity or drama like the glossy magazines tell us to. We can just respectfully say thank you for the time we spent together, the fun we had and for the lessons learned, and then say goodbye. I have come to understand when I need to let go of friendships that are no longer for me and when to hold on to those that nurture me. This is a constant process and that's OK. I used to believe that I 'shouldn't' ever end or say goodbye to a friendship because that would mean I was a 'bad' person or I might hurt others by doing so. But this is just not true. We resonate with different people at different times, we need different people in different moments in our lives and we learn from every single friendship we have. But one thing that they should all have in common is that they should feel nurturing for us and bring positive energy into our lives, not the opposite.

You may want to mark the end of a friendship and consciously draw a line under it by telling the other person how you feel, or you may want to just let it drift naturally. Either is fine, but do both with kindness. Not everyone can be for us or with us forever, most people are not destined to be and that's OK. Friendships get stale and can keep us stuck in the past if we hang on to them when they are clearly not for us anymore.

When You Feel Unappreciated...

> Notice that feeling and your unmet needs.

> Don't let it make you doubt your own worth.

> Understand you don't have to do anything to be valued; you are enough already.

> Have some time and emotional space away from those who do not appreciate you.

> Learn to appreciate yourself: show yourself that, whatever anyone says or does, you always matter.

The way you treat yourself sends a message to others about how they can treat you.

BE AUTHENTIC

Being who you authentically are, loving what you are doing and doing more of it will help you to find your new tribe. Notice coincidences, interactions that you may not have foreseen; be open to meeting new people and make time and space for them. Really take notice of who you are meeting and when. Is there a reason for that? Are you open to trying new things? Are you inspired by that person, does your heart light up when you meet, do you feel valued and heard and free to be yourself?

You never know when a short, fleeting and unremarkable initial encounter is going to turn into an enduring, wonderful and life-changing friendship

How exciting is that?

GATHER SUPPORTERS, NOT ADMIRERS

Don't confuse your tribe with those who always tell you that you are right, who are just trying to please you or who take the easy road of just agreeing all the time. Being a supporter means telling you the truth, even if it is difficult to hear. You want people around you who tell you straight how things really are out of a genuine and honest intention, who have your best interests at heart. This is real support and these are your real cheerleaders.

YOUR TRIBE IS NEVER SET IN STONE

As you grow and change, so your tribe will too. And that's OK. It is a dynamic thing. Just as sports teams change and players come and go according to how the season is going, the same is true of your crew, so don't hang on out of habit or fear or just because you are worried about conflict. If you are being authentic and living your life following your passions, and treating people with kindness and respect, then you will always have supporters around you.

We are not made to live in isolation or to be alone. We are born to connect, to love and to be part of something and alongside someone. That's what makes the world turn.

OVERCOMING OBSTACLES

Tough times come
But they always go away
Until then, all you have to do is just hold on

Stepping up to the challenge of changing things in our lives is not easy. We have got into habits and routines. We are used to being a certain way, allowing others to treat us in a certain way and thinking that our life will carry on in a certain way. Facing up to the challenge to make things different takes courage, energy, determination, motivation and a willingness to try new things.

Whenever we try something new or something hard, we are always going to face obstacles. It's a fact of life. We will fall, fail and falter. And that's OK. The main thing is we try and we keep going until we complete the course. We never know just how we will manage obstacles from looking on from the sidelines; it is only when we start and get going that we realise exactly what we are facing and what we have to overcome.

I used to think the obstacles I faced were outside my control - things that other people did, situations that happened or just life being life. And this is true to a certain extent. However, what we can control and where our power lies is in our ability to make sure we are not being an obstacle to ourselves. We need to get out of the way. Our approach to change can either create more internal obstacles or make the external ones easier to overcome.

What kind of obstacles might you face?

THE STARTING LINE

Resentment about what has happened, blaming others, blaming yourself, guilt and believing nothing can ever be different all keep you standing on the starting line. The starting gun has fired. Life is inviting you to begin, but all you do is stand there, refusing to move, protesting that you never signed up for this and saying that you'll never manage it. Forgiving yourself, forgiving others and forgiving life really helps get you off the starting line. It's an active decision and it takes strength and courage. You don't have to forget, but you can decide not to waste your energy on anger, pain and resentment any longer.

What haven't you forgiven someone for? What are you still holding resentment towards? What still makes you feel angry? For your own sake, not theirs, accept it has happened, take action so it doesn't happen again and let it go. You don't need any extra baggage on your way round the course. Free yourself.

THE ZIP WIRE

I have done a zip wire and I was absolutely terrified of jumping off that platform high up in the trees and letting go of control. I didn't know if I could trust the wire: Would it hold me? Would I be OK? It took all my courage to take a leap of faith and jump off that platform. But when I did, it was amazing. And when I faced the next jump, I didn't even think about it. When we try to have faith that life in some way will step in to hold us, that those who love us will hold us or we will be able to hold ourselves and we will be OK, we can take that leap. Nothing is certain in life, but your ability to take a deep breath, trust and take a chance on yourself can be. If a change scares you then you probably need to make it.

IN THE DITCHES

Deep down in the ditch sits that tricky obstacle of 'It's not fair'. And you are right - life is not fair. You can't change that. But you can accept it as a fact and try to work with it. If you don't, you are going to be stuck down there in that deep, dark ditch with no way up and out. Even if life is not fair, work on being fair to yourself by stopping self-criticism, praising yourself, maintaining boundaries in relationships that mean you are treated with respect, and giving yourself a break when you are overwhelmed. Work on these, every single day. Treat yourself how you would treat others.

THE HIGH WALL

Standing at the bottom of the high wall just staring up at it is not going to help you climb it. In the same way, procrastination is not going to get you anywhere. Delaying, postponing or avoiding things from fear of failure or self-doubt is a tricky obstacle to get around. But remember your journey has momentum of its own. You have already started - you cannot go back, you cannot go sideways, so you must go forward. Even if you don't know what to do, just try to do something, however small, to push yourself in the right direction. If you are looking for new opportunities, get out there searching online, get information and ask others what their experiences are. If you are hoping to find a relationship, be open to finding someone, meet people or focus on making yourself happy on your own first. Remember, inaction can be just as destructive as the 'wrong' action.

UNDER THE NET

There is no way you are going to be able to crawl through the mud under that net on your elbows and knees without getting dirty. Perfectionism is not an option. Things will get messy and they will not always be pretty. It is par for the course so expect imperfection. Expect to make mistakes, to fail and to get things wrong. Out of mess can come beauty. If things don't go right, dust yourself off, tell yourself that it is OK, remind yourself of what has gone well in the past and reflect on what you can learn for next time. Don't let yourself sink deeper into the mud of self-criticism, negativity and self-doubt triggered by the illusion of perfection. We all make mistakes.

THE HURDLES

How high are they? What speed do you need to attack them? What's the best approach? How can you get into a rhythm? Problem-solving is a massive part of getting around the course and through the challenge. We can get trapped just focusing on the problems and how hard they are. Being more open to finding solutions helps you find the best way to approach those hurdles and find your way up and over them. Be flexible in your approach to problems, talk them through with others to get ideas, acquire facts and knowledge, use your imagination and think about less obvious solutions.

Navigating the Course

> ❯ Get specific. Break down obstacles into smaller stumbling blocks.

> ❯ Pace yourself. Make your energy last for the entire race.

> ❯ Ask others for help. They may have run the course before.

> ❯ Don't look back. Focus on where you are now.

> ❯ Don't take your eye off the finish line. It's coming.

THE BALANCE BOARD

Navigating your way through challenge is a delicate balance. You want your voice heard about what you want to change and you don't want to sacrifice your values or compromise, but you want to bring people you care about along with you on the journey. When you express yourself to others, make it factual, listen respectfully, state your position calmly, try to understand their point of view and then make your views known. You don't need to fall out.

Carefully balance your energy and your time. Choose how you want to spend your time and focus on your priorities. Overcoming obstacles takes balance and periods of effort and rest. Are you scheduling these in?

Handling Different Viewpoints

> Don't engage with insults.

> Take a deep breath and avoid reacting.

> Share your views calmly. Listen to theirs.

> Make a considered decision.

> Agree to disagree. Don't disagree to agree.

> Don't give away your power by behaving in a way that isn't true to who you are.

> Be open to changing your mind but don't let anyone change you.

Even though these obstacles seem daunting, you'll learn to navigate them with practice and, if you are faced with them again, you'll be able to look them right in the eye, smile and tackle them head on.

When things seem dark, look for
the light

When you feel lost, find someone
who knows the way

When you are weary, take a rest

When you don't know what to do,
know that one day you will

When you feel like it's all too much,
be kind to yourself

FINDING HOPE

Without hope
Nothing is attempted
Nothing can progress
Nothing will be conquered

People sometimes say to me when I talk about hope that I am 'unrealistic' or that I live in an idealistic world that doesn't exist. But I refuse to listen to them. I refuse to give up hope. Because without hope, nothing can change. Hope is something that has got me through some of the worst times in my life and, if you stop and think about it, it has probably done the same for you. Maybe you have been trying to heal a family rift for years; maybe you have tried to make changes in your life to improve your health and well-being, but don't feel you are getting anywhere; maybe your financial situation has taken a turn for the worse or you have lost your job and you can't see a way forward. I want you to know that there is one, and it starts with finding a tiny bit of hope.

Hope is very different from being positive. Telling someone to be positive in the midst of a life challenge is unrealistic and useless. Hope, however, is one of the most realistic and useful things we can find and feel. Because hope is everywhere we look - it's evident when we look back in the past, we can see it in the present and it is what the future offers freely. **Hope is a tool; it is not a concept.** Hope is the bedrock of our well-being. It helps us begin and attempt something tough, it carves out a way for us to keep going through the most difficult of times, and it helps us find an answer to problems that seemed unsolvable. Hope is simply being open to the possibility of something getting better.

Without hope we have nothing. With hope we are open to everything.

Hope is who you are
It is part of the love that you hold for yourself
It is part of the power that you hold within yourself
It may temporarily be hard to find, but you
are never without it
Never stop looking for it, and never give up on the
possibility that things can and will get better

How can you find hope in tough times?

IN SMALL ACTS

Often, we don't take notice of those small acts of kindness, of community - a friend giving us a hug and a squeeze of the hand, a stranger smiling or opening the door for us, reading a good news story - we take them for granted, we brush them off. Instead, we can choose to take notice and focus on all of them. Really absorb what those small acts signify and acknowledge their presence. They will give you hope even in the darkest of moments.

IN NECESSITY

It may take every ounce of strength to find some hope in tough times, but be reassured we have all felt this way at some point in life. When I find it hard to feel hopeful, I think about what will happen if I don't. And the answer for me always comes out the same: that things will get worse. Even if I don't know anything else in that moment, I know that I don't want them to get worse and I don't want to feel worse. I know you don't want this either. You want them to get better and you absolutely deserve to feel better. Hold on to hope and you will once again.

IN NATURE

Nature never fails to deliver hope. From the biggest and most beautiful of sunrises to the tiny strategic crawl of an ant amongst the blades of grass, nature brings the promise of better times. It is constantly evolving and changing; it offers a real sense of balance and perspective and provides comfort and constancy. Nature is hope in 3D. **Plant a seed, water it, look after it, watch it grow and you will find hope again. Hope is part of nature's DNA.**

FROM OTHERS

Sometimes when we can't find hope, even if we dig as deep as we can, those around us can step in and help us find it. People care, they want to help. Just by talking to them, feeling heard and listened to, getting their perspective and them telling you what they love about you can help. **Just the fact that they care and they want to be there for you will help you find that hope again. Love is hope.** And you deserve to feel loved. Get support.

FROM WHAT HAS BEEN

If you look back at your past, you will be able to see that, even in the toughest of times, there was always something to be hopeful about, and that things always did get better even if it took time. Hold on to hope. Create that future because one day you will be able to look back at this current time and you'll see that it did, indeed, get better.

Hope Is...

> A practical tool we can use to help ourselves feel better.

> Realistic; it's life itself.

> What gets us up out of bed every single day.

> What makes us persevere through tough times.

> The driving force behind finding solutions.

> Everything.

Never give up on hope. It is the essence of life. And you are life. It is hope that helps us hold on during a time of crisis; it is hope that makes us persevere and believe that things can be different during challenge; and it is hope that helps us to take courage and take the next step in changing things so they can be better.

STEP 3

Moving Forward

You've survived and got through the crisis. *You've done the work and stepped up to all the challenges.* You've understood why things have happened, you've learned more about yourself and you're clear now about what needs to change. You've been transforming yourself in your cocoon and you are changed. Now it's time for you to break free from that chrysalis, to see how wonderful it can be to fly and show the rest of the world who you are.

It's time to make an active decision to move things in the direction you want with all the power and momentum that what you have been through has brought.

Change is where the magic happens. It is a beautiful thing. It's when you start seeing the results of all your hard work. But, it's also hard going and frustrating. It comes with resistance, obstacles and bumps in the road. It can be painful, disorientating and scary.

You have to be determined, adaptable, resilient and patient. You have to remember all the lessons you have learned and be aware of slip-ups and steps back. You have to be able to tap into where your power truly lies. Thoughts, words and intentions are all very well, but it's what you do now that really matters.

Now is when the 'I will' transforms into the 'I am'. No one can change anything in your life but you. And nothing can be changed without your action.

Moving forward into change is where your power is fully realised. Are you ready to move forward? I know you are.

Your Power

> To leave the past behind.

> To get clear about your present.

> To create your future.

> This is how your power can be truly seen, really heard and viscerally felt.

> Its sparkling magic and its incredible grace.

REVEALING
THE 'HOW'

It's the 'how to' that transforms
dreams into reality
And ideas into actuality

You have the why and the what. Now you need to focus on the how. How do I do it? **It's the 'how' that really gets things done and moves things forward.**

I used to think that believing in yourself was what truly helped us get through life. But I've come to realise that, though self-belief is of course important, it only takes you so far. Belief on its own is woolly, unreliable and vulnerable to sabotage when we are stressed, tired and having a tough day. **Action carries with it a powerful momentum. Action reinforces belief, and that belief gets stronger and stronger the more we take action. And that more resilient belief encourages more action.** They coexist in a beautiful positive feedback loop. We need both, but if I had to choose one as a starting point, I would always choose action.

I am a big believer in the how. Imagine this: you have bought a lovely new, flat-packed bookcase. You know why you need it and how wonderful it will look when fully constructed. You set aside a rainy Saturday afternoon to put it together. You take out all the pieces, only to find there is no instruction booklet. Those pieces are absolutely useless – they can't hold any books, they can't do the job meant for them – all because you don't know how to put them together. **Intentions and words are meaningless unless we know what to do with them and where to take them.** How many times has your partner promised to take out the bins after yet another argument about it, and then it has never happened? After a while you start to not believe a word they say, not just about the bins but maybe other things too. Seeing action builds trust that things can be different, and it's the same in our own lives.

The how is tangible – it's specific. It transforms your 'what' into something real. It makes stuff change. And the more you act and see results, the more you trust that you can change anything you want.

Get clear about your how

PREPARE

Write out a plan, a timetable, draw a sketch, write a list. What is your goal? What is your timeline? How much time are you going to set aside to help you achieve it? Do you need to create more space to get there and how often is that required - daily, weekly, monthly? What information or skills do you need to attain? Where are you going to get these? Who are you going to ask for help? Break everything down into smaller bits.

BE REALISTIC

In order to achieve your goal, you need to be realistic in your planning. We would all like to click our fingers and for everything to change, but rapid, hurried changes do not last. They are at risk of being forgotten, shelved or compromised when life gets busy or self-doubt gets in the way. I am a classic over-promiser and unrealistic goal-setter. I have learned and accepted that about myself, and now I think two or three times before I draw up any plan. Share your plan with someone who has a better sense of time and productivity if you need to. They can help give you the reality check you need and bring you back down to earth.

USE SPECIFIC TOOLS

Just like with that bookcase that needs screwdrivers and nails, so your how needs specific tools. What are yours? Are they mental tools, like mindfulness and problem-solving; emotional tools, like creativity and hobbies; or physical tools, like daily exercise and more sleep? Take time to work out what these bespoke tools are for you. Write them down and use them daily, and notice when to use which tool.

Your Tools For Change

> Choice: When you feel downhearted, demotivated or like giving up, you have a choice: give up or keep going. Once we realise that we can make a difference to how we feel by what we choose to do in that next moment, we find our power.

> Perseverance: Remember your why. Get stubborn. If you keep on keeping on long enough, something, sometime, will change. If you give up, nothing has the chance to be different. Give yourself a chance.

> Balance: There are times when we need to just be where we are, reflect and show patience, and there are times to expand, for action and to move forward. Create a healthy balance between the two.

> Boundaries: Setting boundaries in all areas of your life – your relationships, your work, your friendships, your family and your schedule – is really important. Make them clear, make them firm and maintain them frequently.

> Habits: Good habits can be our best friends when we are trying to change something. Identify which of your daily habits are useful on your mission to move things forward and use them to help you get a VIP fast-track pass to change.

> Love: The love and kindness of others can really help us make changes in our lives. Encouragement, being able to talk about how we feel, getting advice or a simple hug all help us make positive change in our life. Showing ourselves lots of love also works wonders in how easily we can create a new way of being.

HAVE A PLAN B

Even if we prepare and plan, things never go exactly how we want them to go. Have you got a plan B? What obstacles might crop up and what are your options? How can you show some flexibility? What's your plan C? Don't be ashamed of having as many safety nets as it takes: be proud of your plan Z. Adaptability and confidence help us continue with our changes.

THINK DIFFERENTLY

The road to change is rarely a straight, seamless motorway route; it's more likely a windy country road with bumps, potholes, diversions and cows in the middle of the road that refuse to budge. Try to think laterally - using your imagination and getting creative can help you come up with your how. If you are stuck on problem-solving and can only see things in a certain light, take a break from it. Change your environment, go for a run, stop 'trying' to solve it. Ironically, when we stop trying so hard, we are often presented with a solution.

Without the how, there is no such thing as real change.

Adjusting After Change

> Feeling anxious is expected. It's new to you.

> Be around people who help you feel safe and secure.

> Write a list. Get prepared. Get practical.

> Take time to catch up with how things are now.

> Be gentle with yourself. Take it slow. It's a lot to take in.

In each moment we need different things to help us feel better, so choose a different strategy, a different tool. This is where our power lies - learning about ourselves, what we need in each moment and acting on it. This is how we start to learn to trust ourselves, and how we start to trust that we can handle life.

This moment right now needs
your attention

This situation right here needs
your focus

That attention and focus will
determine your future

So right now give both your
absolute all

CUTTING BACK TO GROW AGAIN

Recognise the power of saying 'No'
And the cost of saying 'Yes'

Saying yes has a cost all of its own that we are not often aware of. Saying no has the power to make the changes you want to happen actually happen. It signals to you, to others and to life that you now want something different. **That is the incredible power of saying no.** Say no to things that aren't really what you want, to things that are going to keep you stuck in the past and to things that are going to delay the changes you want to make.

I remember a pivotal time in my life when I wanted to get more balance in my working week. It was something I'd wanted to do for ages, but, in classic fashion, hadn't got around to. Like with so many things, the work schedule I wanted to rebalance was the very thing that was keeping me from having the time to look at how I could make this change. The irony. As soon as I decided to actively free up some time and space in my diary to think about how I could rebalance and started saying no to things that I didn't want anymore, new things and new opportunities started to present themselves to me. That initial 'freeing up' was really scary because I was used to always being busy, so even just seeing the blank days in my diary made me nervous. But, the decision to cut back for a while in order to allow in the new was one of the best decisions I could have ever made.

Just like plants need to be pruned in order to allow new growth, so we need to cut back in a similar way in our lives when we want to invite new things in. Pruning helps plants to stay healthy, to be shaped into a new form; it stops them getting out of control and showcases their best bits. But it also needs to be done at the right time, with a clear idea about what you are cutting back and why you are doing it. If you are new to horticulture it can be pretty scary because that plant looks really bare and like it will never, ever grow again. But, with time and patience, it does. In fact, it grows back bigger and better. It's the same when you start saying no to things that you no longer want and when you cut back to free up time and space. Your life expands in ways you could never have imagined. Be prepared to sit in that uncomfortable and nerve-wracking 'pruned' zone for a while.

How to hold your nerve when you're cutting back

IT WILL FEEL SCARY

When you start to cut back, you will doubt yourself. Are you doing the right thing? Maybe other people are right. Maybe it would be 'safer' just to go back to how things were. Have you gone too far? I had all of these worries, and that was before I even considered other people's judgements and opinions. Take a breath, remember why you are doing this and what things were like before. Do you really want to 'go back'? What's the worst-case scenario if you just held on for a while? Something needs to change. Know that doubt will be a constant companion for a while, and that's to be expected.

IT'S A PROCESS

Cutting back is about stepping away from things that no longer serve your vision for your future or aren't aligned with who you are becoming. But discernment is a very important caveat. Don't go extreme and say no to everything. Choose a couple of things in your different life areas that you want to cut back on as a priority. Work on those first. Pilot those changes for a couple of months and then review things. Are things working how you wanted them to or do you need to change things up again? It is a gradual and evolving process. See it like a scientific experiment – change one variable at a time and then assess, respond as you need to and assess again. It shouldn't be done all in one short, sharp blow. You'll just get stressed out and will be more likely to lose confidence in the whole process.

Deciding What to Cut Back

> Write a list of all the things you want to let go of.

> Write down all the new things you want to invite in.

> Get your diary out, have your phone at hand, write the words 'Say No' on a Post-it note and put it on your bathroom mirror or in your wallet.

> And then slowly but surely make things happen.

TIMING IS EVERYTHING

Tune into your intuition, your sense of knowing. When is the right time to cut back on certain things in different areas of your life and when isn't? Even if you desperately want something to change and that's top of your list, don't force it and don't get fixated on it. If a change you are trying to make doesn't seem to be flying right now, then maybe you need to put it on hold until it does, and in the meantime focus on another. There may also be practical, outside factors that will determine the timing. For example, financial responsibilities, logistics of where you live and your daily routine, or family commitments that are imminent. I know it is a cliché, but things do happen at the right time. If they aren't happening right now, it doesn't mean they won't and it doesn't mean you can't do the groundwork to help prepare for when the time is right. How many times have you looked back and wished you had not stressed so much about a situation, but instead trusted the timing?

FILTER OTHER PEOPLE'S OPINIONS

You are the expert in your life and in your world. You can certainly listen to what others think about what you are cutting out or stepping away from, but, at the end of the day, it is your responsibility to move your life in the direction that feels right for you. It is as simple as that. That is where your power lies. So, say 'thank you' to others for their opinion, but, if it does not resonate with you, let it go, move on and do what you need to do anyway. Don't let their opinions, judgements and projection of their own life limitations affect your desire to change something for yourself. They are not you. Beware those vocalised opinions that exactly match your own fears and worries - they can trigger a big reaction.

Some people will question your decisions
Some will make you doubt yourself
Some may even try to stop you in your tracks
But if it feels right to you, then it's your
'mistake' to make

It's tempting to leave things exactly as they are and always have been because they are 'OK', but what if they could be more than OK? Maybe OK was good enough for you before, but is it anymore? Do you want more from your life now? What if things could be remarkable, extraordinary or amazing? **Making the decision to see if and how things could be different is a courageous one, but if you don't take it, you will never, ever know. Don't make OK your default.**

SAYING GOODBYE

There are so many ways to say goodbye
And so many ways to avoid saying it, too
A goodbye is a hello to something new
And something different

Change does not come easily and it doesn't happen overnight. Sometimes you will feel like you are going backwards, sometimes life will present you with more lessons and sometimes you can't always put into action the strategies you know are helpful. It will sometimes feel like it is one step forward, and two back. Like a back-and-forth, push-pull, cat-and-mouse game.

Be prepared for a tug of war between the old and the new. Sometimes the old will look like it's winning; sometimes the new will take the advantage. Don't worry, tension has to be there so the new can pull and the tug of war can be won. Be prepared, get your team ready, brace yourself and conserve your energy.

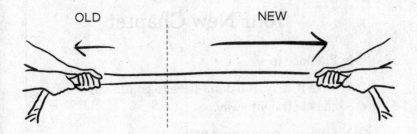

OLD

NEW

The old is not your enemy to be feared, rather it is a gentle reminder of what you don't want.

Every time it pulls on that rope, you get a reminder of the past and you can get stronger in your resolve to pull things in the new direction. Every pull from the old lets us know with stronger clarity why this needs to happen. Doing anything different or new is uncomfortable. You are stepping out of your comfort zone, and the old has momentum already behind it and on its side. Work out how you can reduce the past's advantage. Start with a clear plan, with energy, with the belief that you can do this, with strategies ready to go and with supporters on your side.

Swinging back and forth from the new into the old for a while is no bad thing. Those reminders of the past and falling back into old ways that we want to leave behind can actually strengthen the new, establish it on solid foundations and ensure it finds its permanent home.

Your New Chapter

> Embrace it.

> Take it easy. You don't have to go full steam ahead straight away.

> Envision your future path.

> Emotions can come up from old situations. Don't let them define or limit you.

> Be excited. You get to define your new chapter.

Change means letting some things go... Saying goodbye to the old, to things, people, situations and dynamics that have been with us for a long time, maybe for many years. With any goodbye, even if it is us who has chosen to say goodbye and it's something we have been anticipating for a long time, there is always an element of sadness and a sense of anxiety, loss and disorientation. But, with every goodbye, we are offered the gift of reflecting on what has happened - the good things and the not-so-good things - and on everything we have achieved or faltered at.

However hard the end of something can be, know that without a goodbye there cannot be a hello. Hello to the new, to exciting opportunities, to unknown adventures and to mind-blowing discoveries. Letting things go means things can change now. And our job with any goodbye is to leave with dignity, with gratitude and with grace.

How can you leave the old chapter gracefully and step into the new one with less trepidation?

WITH FORGIVENESS

If we don't forgive others or let go of resentment or anger towards a past situation, then we are only going to take that heavy burden with us into the next chapter. And make no mistake, it is a burden and it can block us from starting anew. **Forgiveness sets you free from the past and stops whatever happened from controlling your thoughts, your emotions and your actions.** This doesn't mean allowing the situation that was painful to repeat or allowing others to behave in the same way in the future. It is saying that you are taking back control. Actively forgive others and yourself for what has been so you can move into what can be. If you find this hard, ask yourself how holding on to blame makes you feel. What does it limit you doing? What does it actually achieve? Who is really suffering from holding on to it? How would you live your life without it? It might feel good to hold on to resentment in the short term, but it will never give you the peace or freedom you are looking for.

ON GOOD TERMS

A goodbye should be just that - 'good'. Leave things on good terms, whatever has happened. This way you can hold your head high and leave with dignity, having behaved in a way that is in line with your values and who you are. However the other person acts or however they receive your goodbye, you can still be proud of yourself for how you handled it. Don't allow your power to be hijacked by something or someone else's actions. Respond don't react. Stay true to who you are. That is where your power lies.

SEEKING CLOSURE

If there are things that need to be said, spoken about or sorted out, get closure. Write a letter, send a text, apologise, understand, ask. If there is something niggling you deep down that still grates, or bothers you or you feel uncomfortable about, get on it. Closing the door properly on something allows you to focus on opening a new one, without a draught from the past blowing chills past you every now and again for evermore.

HAVING NO REGRETS

Everything that has happened has been for a reason, although this is often hard to see and understand when you are deep down in it. You can learn from every experience you have had and you can take these lessons with you into the next phase of your life. Regrets stop us from moving on and keep us revisiting the past. And if we haven't sorted through them and seen them for what they are, they also affect our reaction to events in our future. Let's say a friend has let you down by being late or cancelling at the last minute, and you get triggered into a huge argument or just ignore them completely. If you find yourself responding in a way that is out of proportion to what has actually happened, it could well be because you still have unfinished business from the past that you haven't learned lessons from. **Allow yourself to act differently now rather than waste time on regrets. There is nothing you can do to change the past, but you can absolutely change the present, and what you do in the present creates your future.** The present is where your power lies. Regrets are like the worst kind of hangover.

BEING GRATEFUL

Gratitude is a great tool that helps us reframe things and get some perspective. Choose five things from that life experience that you are grateful for. Sometimes the 'worst' things we experience turn out to be the most powerful and life-changing moments. Try to be grateful for all of it.

How to Leave Old Chapters Behind

> Reflect on what you have learned.

> Reframe what you have been through.

> Regrets shouldn't get in your way.

> Recognise that reluctance to let go keeps you stuck in the past.

> Reset what you want to do and who you want to be.

> Realise that everything changes so this will too.

Goodbyes are never easy and can be painful, but hanging on to things when they are no longer for us is harder and even more painful.

Let Go...

> Of who you once were.

> Of how things have been.

> Of who is no longer for you.

> Of things that no longer serve you.

> Of things that have held you back.

> Of people who have made you feel small.

You're making space for something else now.

Appreciating what you have now is the fastest, easiest and most direct route to happiness. Don't take the long, arduous and never-ending route of waiting for someone or something to make you happy, or you could be waiting for a very, very long time.

CHANGING THE 'UNCHANGEABLE'

There's a lot of change to work through
A lot of information to digest
A lot of fear, worry and anxiety to process
A lot of uncertainty to hold
So, make sure you give yourself
a lot of kindness, gentleness and understanding

It feels great to be able to get our teeth into something that we want to change and to actually see that happen. But what about when we realise it is going to be harder to change something than we could ever have thought? That, in fact, it might never change, no matter how hard we work at it, how long we try for and how much effort we put in?

It's so important to understand that there are some things you will not ever be able to change: other people, what happened in the past, what will happen to us in the future, situations and events outside of our control. On the surface, this sounds very negative and defeatist, and that's how I used to see it. But, it's true and, when we understand this, we reclaim our power. Though we can't change certain things, what we can change is how we respond to them, because that is always in our control. How we perceive others and experience things that happen to us can change too. Focus on where you have power and control, and put your energy there. In this way, **even the seemingly once 'unchangeable' can be changed.**

Transport yourself just for a minute into a tense, stressful family Christmas, or an equivalent nightmare. Maybe that's a difficult interaction with another person in your life, your boss, a work colleague, an ex-partner, a friend. You know - those dates in your calendar that you dread, try your best to avoid, but always end up having to have some contact with. You have tried for years to get along with this person, you've tried different strategies, you've bent over backwards to compromise, you've lost your temper - but nothing has worked. And now you are right back in the same old dynamic. You can't change who they are, their behaviour or how they approach the situation. **But, remember, our relationship with everyone and everything is not a one-way traffic system. It's always two-way.** If you change your part in this dynamic and the kind of energy you are bringing to that chat or interaction, there is opportunity for the interaction to change. The old way of doing things is destabilised. That other person will have to find someone else to argue with or some other way to keep that energy of conflict alive and get their kicks. Whatever happens, you are not giving your power away by being swept into the old dynamic.

Today you deserve to realise
It's not all on you
It's not all up to you
But what you can do
Do

I often treat interactions with people who I find challenging as an opportunity for me to evolve as a person, a bit like 'spiritual practice' - I take time to notice the old thoughts and feelings arising when they do, try to take a breath and step out of them so I can choose to respond differently. And afterwards, I review things: have I evolved a bit more or enough to feel differently or to handle the situation differently? Sometimes I can do it, sometimes I can't - and that's OK. It is like building a muscle; it can be done with slow and steady patience.

If you want to change a difficult dynamic

BE OBJECTIVE

When situations are old, stuck and rigid, it's easy to put on the same old pair of blurry glasses and just see it through these. Take a new look at an old situation with a fresh pair of eyes. Maybe you have blamed someone else entirely in the past; maybe you have judgements about them and opinions that are clouding your perspective. What are you bringing to the situation? Look at what the other person or the circumstances are bringing. Is there a good reason they are behaving that way? Are they scared or under pressure? How are those patterns triggering each other and creating stress or tension? When you change your perspective, the situation and dynamic will change in some shape, manner or form - it has to. When you truly try to put yourself in that other person's shoes, can you approach them with kindness and understanding? How could this change the dynamic? Ask yourself: do you truly want things to change? There is no point paying lip service to this. You have to truly want it for anything to be different.

DIG DEEP

You may have to ask yourself some tough questions and dig into some deep emotions to understand how the dynamic has been formed and what is keeping it going. What are you looking for? Is it approval, love or validation? Is it to feel heard or to have your boundaries accepted? If the other person is unable or unwilling to give this to you, can you give it to yourself, or look elsewhere for support? What is your unmet need that is causing you emotional pain? What is it about the situation that makes you want it to change? Just like we need to dig up the roots of a weed to truly get rid of it for good, so we need to do the same in seemingly 'unchangeable' situations.

ACCEPT IT

Realising that you are banging your head against a brick wall and wasting your energy trying to change a situation that is clearly not going to change now, or perhaps ever, is very freeing. It is not a defeat and it is not saying you are powerless; quite the opposite. It allows you to approach the situation without the pressure of 'it needs to change' and without energising the already difficult dynamic with all that unseen pressure. Acceptance helps to diffuse and de-energise the situation. When there is more acceptance and more space around a situation, there is more opportunity for it to potentially change because it's not being held quite so tightly in place.

RECOGNISE YOU ALWAYS HAVE SOME CONTROL

There is always something you can do, however small and seemingly insignificant. Can you change your attitude or your expectations? Can you change your perception of it being a 'problem' to just being an experience or a learning lesson? Can you make practical preparations and take steps that will open up new avenues for you to move out of an 'unchangeable' situation? If you feel powerless in a situation or a dynamic, never stop looking for what you can control. It might be removing yourself from that situation. It might be just staying silent or it might be smiling politely while you take a deep breath. It may not feel like action or that 'powerful', but it is. You are doing something different to try to make something different happen. You never know how a small step can slowly start an avalanche of change.

Find your power in an 'unchangeable' situation or dynamic. It is always there even if it is hard to see and even if it takes a lot of practice and patience. There is always something that can be changed. No excuses.

How to Deal with the 'Unchangeable'

> Identify what you can change and do that.

> Identify what others could change and ask them to do that.

> Don't be discouraged – it will take time and hard work.

> Don't get frustrated and give up – that won't help you.

> Accept what you can't change and move on.

At the end of every single day, try to let things go, be proud of yourself and find something that makes you smile. **You are doing amazingly well. That is undeniable.**

FEELING ALONE

The only person you will be with for
the whole of your life is you
So, you are never alone
This is where your company and your
comfort can be found

One of the hardest and most painful feelings we can feel
is to feel alone. We're human and we need connection;
we need to feel like we belong and that someone under-
stands us. **When we make changes in our lives, we will
undoubtedly at times feel alone, because we're changing
the rules.**

Every game comes with a set of rules on how to
play - sometimes they are written down officially and
sometimes they are more just tradition. In all of our relationships, there is a set of conscious and subconscious
'rules' too. Our interactions with others, over time, form a
bespoke collection of behaviours and responses that both
'players' are used to; they know how to play the game

and they know how the other 'player' - you - is going to play. When we change, people around us get confused, disorientated and sometimes even feel threatened or abandoned. They don't like having the 'rules' changed halfway through the game. The relationship dynamic was an unwritten contract that you entered into and have been abiding by for a long time, and they feel like it was working well, so why change it? They may get angry, try to resist the new dynamic or behave in ways that make you feel very much out on your own, or even blame you. And even if they don't, you may still feel alone because you're also trying to work out what the new rules of the game are right now.

I want you to know - that's OK. There will be resistance, so expect it and don't get taken by surprise. But don't interpret that resistance as a sign that you are doing something 'wrong' or are on the 'wrong path'. And don't let it stop you from making the changes you feel you need to make in your life. Just see it for what it is. A change.

Making changes in your life will cause stress, tension and challenge. But that doesn't mean you shouldn't make them.

It's more about how you handle it

SEE IT FOR WHAT IT IS

If loneliness and feelings of abandonment or exclusion come up, it doesn't necessarily mean you are making wrong decisions or that you are wrong. These feelings are likely coming from you stepping out of your usual patterns that you have been so familiar with. Don't let fear of feeling alone stop you from making your change if, deep in your heart, you know it's in your best interests. **Make fear your servant, not your ruler. Remember, it is your life, no one else's.**

When You Are Feeling Lonely

> Be good company for yourself.

> Pick up the phone, get out and about and connect with others.

> Remember that you are not alone in feeling lonely - we all feel like this from time to time.

> ❯ Try to identify what is missing right now: activity, kindness, understanding? How can you get that unmet need met?

> ❯ Get outside and find your company there – life is always active, busy and full.

IT WON'T BE FOREVER

With time, those around you are more likely to come around to the changes you are making once they see that you are happier and your life is better. Their trust and confidence will grow. Even if it doesn't, it's best not to fall into the trap of blaming them for their reaction and creating more separation. They, like you, are just trying to do their best and reorientate. And, remember, your self-confidence and trust in the changes you are making will grow, so you may not even need their approval anymore. Either way, you will feel better and you won't feel so alone.

KEEP YOUR ALLIES CLOSE

You will have allies – those people who understand you and understand why you are making these changes. You need to talk to them about how you are feeling, the kind of resistance you are coming up against and the doubts that are rearing their head. They can support you, remind you of why you are making changes and offer a different perspective. Write a list of your allies and have them on speed dial during a period of change. Arrange to meet up with them regularly and really listen to their advice. You may need some space from those who don't understand or who criticise or make you doubt yourself, especially during the early stages of making your changes.

SPOT THE SIGNS

Resistance from others may come in different forms. They may tell you that you are 'wrong', that you 'don't know what you are doing' or that they know better. They may try to scare or frighten you with worst-case scenarios of doom and gloom. They may cut you off completely, get moody or sulky, or try all kinds of behaviours to manipulate your decision-making. Don't fall for it. Think about what the repercussions will be for you and your life if you listened to them. Not only would you stay stuck, but you would also reinforce the message that you can't be trusted to make your own decisions, that you can't trust yourself. You will be giving your power away to them. And you can't let that happen. Politely decline the invitation to get involved in their drama and gently hold firm.

BEING ALONE VERSUS BEING LONELY

Being alone doesn't mean you have to feel lonely. Find things to do that nurture that meaningful connection you can have with yourself. Look after yourself, take time to comfort yourself, say reassuring things to yourself, do things you enjoy and that help you express who you are. Get to know yourself better. Be your own best friend, your biggest supporter and your most cherished company. You don't need to filter anything out. You just need to let self-acceptance and self-confidence in. You are your best ally. There are real gifts in sometimes having periods of time in solitude and being alone. It is all part of you finding yourself, understanding yourself and learning to love yourself more.

Setting your own rules in the game of life is one of the most powerful things you can do. Whatever happens, at least you know that you did it your way, and no one else's. **Your life journey is yours to create. Your rules are yours to make.**

Be Your Own Best Friend

> Understand your fears and be gentle with them.

> Listen, smile and encourage yourself.

> Ask yourself often 'How am I really doing?'

> Tell yourself you are not alone. You have you, and always will.

> Spend some meaningful time with yourself, doing things you love, that bring you joy and make you laugh.

> Show yourself that you are loved. Buy flowers, rest your head on a soft pillow, romance yourself.

OLD HABITS DIE HARD

Habits are hard to break
But it's harder to live with ones that are getting in
the way of you living the life you want

No change is ever easy, even if it is one that we want. Why? Because of our habits. They can be the hardest things to break. But it can be done.

Our brains have evolved to make the things we do a lot easier. They form things called 'habit loops'. Something happens and acts as a trigger, we react to this trigger (with thoughts, feelings or actions) and then we get a reward for that behaviour. The more we play out and engage with this loop, the stronger it gets, until eventually it becomes automatic. We do the same old thing without even thinking about it, and at lightning speed. This frees up time for our brain to focus on processing new things and the more complex decisions. Our habits are just like background software systems on our computers running all the time and taking up a tiny bit of the battery. These habit loops become ingrained over time and this is why habits take so much resolve, energy and awareness to break and why, if you want to make changes in your life, you will encounter obstacles and roadblocks.

Sometimes these roadblocks will just be a set of traffic lights where you need to wait for a couple of minutes, but sometimes they will be major roadworks and diversions that take you off your route completely. Remember, though, if you persevere, you will eventually get closer to your destination. Whatever you do, don't just give up, turn around and go home.

Every time you notice that you have hit a roadblock and every time you realise that you've been taken on a diversion *and* you find your way around them, that old habit loop weakens and the new habit loop that you are trying to create is strengthened. So, keep going. Who wants to be a passive player in their lives, controlled by automatic reactions? **Rather than being 'controlled', don't you want control over your behaviours? Don't you want to be the authority in your own life? Well, you can be, and changing your habits allows you to do this.**

How to get back in control

KNOW YOUR ENEMY

Old habits aren't exactly your enemy, more like a misguided opponent. Remember, they once served you in some way. You created and reinforced them for a reason - to keep you safe, in familiar territory and feeling comfortable. It's just that now you have realised they aren't helpful anymore and you can see things in a different light. You have changed and they need to, too. Get clear on what your existing habits are, what the trigger, the response and the reward has been, and what new habit loop is that you want to form. For example, let's say you are trying to get more work-life balance. In the past you have kept your email notifications on your phone on loud. Whenever your phone pinged (the trigger) you would check email, no matter what the time was (the response), and reply. You would feel in control and not worry that you hadn't replied (the reward). Now, notice that ping, notice the automatic behaviour of reaching for your phone, breathe, step out of it and choose differently - don't check your emails. Sound simple? Well, try it - you'll realise that it's not. But it can be done. It's all about awareness.

GET PRACTICAL

Start to create your new habit loop and practise rein-
forcing it. Take practical steps to make the new habit loop
easier to fall into. For example, to help you with those
emails, turn off notifications, put your phone away, put
on an auto out of office and keep busy so you are not
just scrolling through your phone. Put in place a series of
steps to create more space and time between the trigger
and the response. Schedule in time, invest effort, make
mental space and have strategies that can help you break
the cycle. Create a new behaviour to replace the old one.
When you now experience the same trigger, what is going
to be your new response and what's going to be your new
reward? Team up with others who are trying to do the
same and you can encourage each other to keep going or
step in when you feel one of you is slipping back.

BE PERSISTENT

A small something is better than a big fat nothing.
Don't let yourself have a 'day off'. Even if only in a small
way, riding that wave works. Momentum works. Make
a promise to yourself, tick off something that you have
changed about that habit loop every day. Let's say you
want to do something active every day and you are doing
really well for the first two weeks, but then you have a
day when it's raining, it's cold or you feel tired. Even if

you don't go for a run outside or do your usual cycle, do some stretching, hoover your living room or clean your bathroom. Any activity is better than none at all. Your intention is still being honoured and the momentum is still maintained, so it's more likely that you'll get back to it the following day. Promises are not just things that we make and try to keep for other people. They are things we need to make and keep for ourselves too.

HAVE SAFETY NETS

You will have tough days when you slip up or you feel like you are going backwards. That's OK. Make a plan for these tough days. Exactly how are you going to manage them? What safety nets do you have in place – a friend to talk to, a self-care kit, a reminder of your why on the fridge door, a positive affirmation you can say to yourself? Tell others about what you are trying to achieve so you are held to account in a gentle way by those who care about you. It's these safety nets that will catch you when you fall.

Affirmations for Today

> 'I know what to do.'

> 'I believe in myself.'

> 'I am doing the best I can, and that's enough.'

> 'I will get there in the end.'

> 'I can do this.'

> 'I won't ever give up.'

REWARD YOURSELF

We don't break or make habits by being unkind or critical about ourselves. In fact, that's a sure-fire route to giving up on making positive changes. I always remember that the teachers I worked hardest for at school were the teachers who I respected, who were fair and who encouraged and supported me, not the ones who were critical, unkind or dictatorial. It is the same when you are learning to do things differently. New habits are best formed by reward, encouragement and lots of praise. Draw a visual goal and reward timeline. Get clear what your daily reward will be and how you will treat yourself when you get to a major milestone. Will it be a new lip gloss, a day off work, a new bit of tech or a small party with friends? Treat yourself, it will keep you going.

Have your old habits created your life so far? Most likely, yes. But, now you know about them, you can be free of them. Create new habits. They'll help you create your new future.

Déjà Vu

If you've been here before...

> Remember what you learned before: what worked and what didn't.

> Remember what helped you make a breakthrough.

> Remember, even if things feel the same, you are very different.

> Remember sometimes we need to do things over to make them last.

> Remember there's no shame in taking a step back, in order to take a couple forward.

FACING DOWN DOUBT

Doubt what you do
Doubt what you think
But never doubt who you are

Self-doubt commonly raises its ugly head during critical times of change. It is inevitable. We can't change that, but we can change how well prepared we are for it, and how we deal with it when it turns up. Our job is not to try to eliminate it - that's impossible. Our job is to handle it and not let self-doubt turn into self-sabotage.

We know what our dreams and goals are. But doubt can stop us in our tracks. You know the feeling - those times when you have made a few small, positive changes and, finally, everything seems to be going well. Then, out of nowhere, you start to think, 'What's the catch?', 'It can't be this good', 'It can't be this easy', 'Surely something is going to go wrong'. And the self-doubt turns into self-sabotage and then into full-on imposter syndrome: 'I don't deserve this', 'This happens to other people, not me', 'Someone somewhere is going to realise soon that I can't do this'.

Where do all these pesky thoughts come from? Usually from our belief that we don't deserve good things to happen to us; a fundamental belief that we are not good enough. We need to face them down before they make us feel like an imposter in our own lives.

How can you head off self-doubt and self-sabotage?

STOP CARRYING THINGS THAT AREN'T YOURS

A lot of the doubtful thoughts we have are not actually ours - they are things that other people have said to us in the past that we have believed, picked up and carried for years. Remember that 'story' that was written for you? Well, who is narrating it? Ask yourself whose voice it is that keeps telling you that you are not good enough or that you are going to make a mistake. Write down these thoughts when they come into your mind. You might notice that the words and phrases sound like they come from your mum or dad, or your sibling, or a teacher from your school, or a critical boss. Do you want to take notice of them anymore? That voice doesn't have to rule your life or ruin your dreams. Once you can see these beliefs are not yours to own or carry anymore, and in fact they never were, you can set them down.

NOTICE AND ACT FAST

Doubt will always arise, but it doesn't have to be a permanent fixture. We have a choice to just allow it to be fleeting in nature only. How much power we give it over us is ours to determine. Doubt doesn't have to turn into sabotage, and sabotage doesn't have to turn into full-on imposter syndrome and ruin things. We need to try to act speedily to stop it in its tracks as soon as we notice it. Our brains have a brilliant but annoying ability to take a thought, expand it, ruminate on it, make it more complicated and overanalyse everything. If we deal with doubt too slowly, it will run amok. So, when you notice thoughts of self-doubt, practise letting it pass through without attaching to it or following it, use an affirmation to reassure yourself that you are more than good enough or get up and get busy to take yourself away from it.

DIFFERENTIATE BETWEEN USEFUL DOUBT AND SELF-DOUBT

Self-doubt that stops us from following our dreams usually comes from a place of low self-esteem and is rarely of any benefit. Useful doubt, however, can help us to rationally weigh up data and information. It helps us question, reflect and think logically about the choices we have. It can help us to go cautiously and carefully and make good decisions. When doubt rears its head, listen to it, but if it starts on you or your self-worth, or gets personal, stop listening and tell it politely that you are not interested.

RECOGNISE THE SOUND OF SELF-SABOTAGE

Self-sabotaging thoughts include extreme words or phrases like 'can't', 'never been able to', 'don't deserve' or 'won't happen for me'. When you think about the changes you are trying to make, what words are you using? Pay attention. Notice your thoughts and words and iden-tify any sabotaging ones. Replace them with 'can', 'will be able to', 'definitely deserve' and 'can happen for me'. |It is powerful.

Today:

Reduce the volume on worry.

Close the door on fear.

Walk away from doubt.

Instead:

Turn up kindness.

Turn on the music.

Turn towards the sun.

Self-doubt is not your enemy, but can actually be a friend in an excellent disguise. Every time you manage to face it down and head it off, you claim an important and significant victory. **You can win your battle with doubt, you can win the war against sabotage and you can take your imposter prisoner. You can show yourself how powerful you are.**

Withstanding Waves of Challenge

> Trust your ability to stand with both feet firmly in the sand.

> Work out how each wave's impact can be absorbed.

> When stronger waves come, make sure you dig deep.

> Learn to work with the wave and not against it.

> The waters will calm eventually, so be patient.

BEING FLEXIBLE

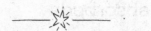

Take things day by day
That's all any of us can do
If we just do this
The days will one day get better

Change is never linear. Instead, it wiggles left, right, up, down, stopping, starting and sometimes circling around and around. Like life itself, even if we know what we want and how we might achieve it, it never happens just as we planned. The very process of change itself requires us to change things up, to be flexible. We have to be adaptable about our 'what' and adjustable about our 'how'.

Don't fall into the trap of rigidly trying to make it all happen exactly how you think it should, and by doing so miss golden opportunities that might even be more in your best interests. **You have to get comfortable with changing the 'change' itself. I know, it's all a bit meta.**

Change is more effective and efficient when we are able to be innovative with problem-solving skills, think outside the box, know when and where to refocus our energy and sometimes even to delay or let go of some of the changes we thought we had to make for the time being.

Problem-solving...

> Reduces anxiety because you find solutions.

> Helps you get your worries out of your mind.

> Works better with a 'can do' attitude.

> Is a life skill that you can learn.

> Helps you trust that you can cope with whatever comes your way.

Flexibility builds self-trust and resilience. And we need both of these when it comes to managing periods of transition and change. And just like practising yoga builds physical flexibility, we can practise how we handle change to build our life flexibility.

There are positions and poses that you can manoeuvre into on your journey of change

DOWNWARD-FACING DOG: STRETCHES AND CENTRES

Life will test us. And sometimes there is a good reason for this. It's trying to 'stretch' us to prevent us from just sitting in our comfort zone and doing what we have always done, because life knows we are more than we are allowing ourselves to be and we are stronger than we could ever know. Expect periods of sometimes extreme challenge when you are trying to change something. Prioritising sleep, rest and being selective about what you do during these times can help. We need to feel grounded, centred and secure to get through these times. Use grounding techniques like deep-breathing exercises, get your bare feet out there on the grass or listen to nostalgic music to remind you that you are safe and to help you find your bearings.

WARRIOR 1 AND WARRIOR 2: FOCUSES AND STRENGTHENS

Remember that our focus and strength is sometimes built from having to learn our lesson more than once - sometimes twice over and sometimes more. When life 'gets in the way' of your planned changes, don't resist; instead, focus on what you can change right now, and focus on what changes you can make to your planned change. Don't retreat. Adopt courage, hard work, discipline and patience. Think about the 'warriors' from books, films or fairy tales - they know how to win through in the end and they don't rush in their quest. Be more like them - unleash your inner warrior.

CORPSE POSE: CALMS AND RELAXES

Having to change your change can cause you to feel anxious, fearful and scared. That's natural - you have worked long and hard to get to this point and you now want it to happen. But, remember, everything in its own time. Right now, you need to be your own best friend and find ways of calming yourself. Where can you find comfort? Is it in talking to others, in nature or in self-expression or creativity? Is it in a hug, a soft blanket or a swim? Problem-solving, adapting to circumstances and making new decisions are all best done in a calm and relaxed state. You'll find your answers there.

Whatever tomorrow brings, you will be OK
Be just a little malleable, mouldable, supple and pliant
And not too rigid, set, fixed or unyielding
Go with whatever comes your way and work with it,
not against it

MOUNTAIN POSE: BALANCES AND ALIGNS

Check in with yourself regularly to see how things are going in this whirlwind of changing plans. When we have to change our change, we can get taken off course and distracted. How are you feeling? Are you still maintaining a good work-life balance? Are you balancing change with enough constancy and familiarity? Are you constantly realigning your intentions, decisions and actions with your goals and with the change you want to make? Are you turning down the noise on those around you who may be filling you with doubt or who aren't supportive?

CHILD'S POSE: RESETS AND RESTORES

Changing the change can be tiring. Reset yourself. Restore your mental and emotional energy levels with good sleep, doing things that make you feel more joy, writing, creating art, being in nature, cuddling your pets and laughing more. Have a weekend break, take a day off, do something totally new. You need this to help you stay committed to your journey and keep you on your path.

Changing the 'Change'

› Take a breath. Keep calm. Don't panic.

› Ask others to help you create different plans of action to reach your goals.

› Move with the times. Don't get stuck in the past.

› Things may even work out better than you could ever have imagined or hoped for. Be open to this.

› When it all settles, make sure you have a break. Change is tiring.

Flexibility when our 'change' changes helps us get through it in one piece and actually reach our destination. **Like the branch of a tree in a storm, unless it moves with the wind it will break. We have to learn to go with life not against it.**

CELEBRATING YOUR WINS

Praise yourself
Treat yourself
Acknowledge all you have been through

Nothing good ever comes from criticism or being hard on yourself. You might have been told or believe that unless you keep on at yourself, you will never get anything done or you won't achieve anything. This is completely untrue. When we have gone through a time of crisis, challenge and change, we deserve to and absolutely need to take time and space to celebrate our wins and reward ourselves.

The rewards that we get from the actual changes that we make may be enough – the good feeling from changing up our sleep and exercise habits, for example – but there is often a lag between sowing our seeds of change and reaping the harvest. Without treats, praise and rewards in the meantime, it's tempting for us to give up. We can get demotivated and we can get a skewed view of life as an existence of pure struggle.

It shouldn't all be about the hard work. It also needs to be about your recognition of the hard work, you marking it and you celebrating it. You need to make a fuss of yourself for everything that you have coped with and managed, give yourself validation for just being you and throw yourself a massive party.

What does that party look like?

TAKING A MOMENT

We get so obsessed with moving on to the next thing, that we often overlook and neglect what we have achieved. We ignore the seemingly 'small' achievements, but add those up - they are huge. I know it's sometimes hard to do this, but take a moment to stop, think about what you have been through, what you have coped with and where you are now. Remember those small moments in time when you wanted to give up or almost fell back into that old habit, but didn't and you made a better choice for yourself. Those moments are massive. Write them down. I promise you will be impressed beyond belief.

SPEAK POSITIVELY

Congratulating yourself matters. Reward yourself for everything you have done – the 'good', the 'bad' and everything in between. Speaking well about yourself is not arrogant or egotistical; it is just you being fair to yourself. Say well done, say it often and say it with meaning. Make sure your thoughts are full of the kind of words you would use to speak to a small child who you are proud of and who you love beyond belief.

Today's challenge:

- ☐ Say one kind thing to yourself every time you see your reflection in a mirror.
- ☐ See what a difference it can make to how you feel.
- ☐ Notice how it can change the way you think about yourself.
- ☐ Observe how new opportunities open up for you.
- ☐ And repeat.

REWARD YOURSELF

There is science behind this common sense. Our brains respond to reward and we are more likely to continue making our changes. Whether it is a small treat or a big one, it really doesn't matter. Give yourself the validation you need: a takeaway, a new outfit, a day off or a trip to your favourite show... whatever floats your boat.

MARK IT

Get people together and let them celebrate you. Let everyone know your achievements and make some noise. You deserve it. Our own self-validation is great, but we are human and we need validation from others too. The people who truly care and who love you will want to mark your achievements, and people always love an excuse for a party. Don't hide your achievements or wait to celebrate. Life is too short.

ACCEPT COMPLIMENTS

We can be very quick to refute compliments or dismiss them, to say 'Oh it's nothing', to hide our light. Sometimes we feel we don't deserve it, we are not good enough, we don't like the attention or we think we might come across as arrogant or 'big-headed'. When someone offers you a compliment, listen and really hear it, acknowledge it by saying thank you and let it sink in. Don't brush over it, don't interrupt it, don't devalue yourself by rejecting it. Recognise you absolutely deserve to be praised. Accepting compliments is a great habit to develop.

This is your party. Make sure you accept the invitation, dress up, get there early and give yourself a gift of recognition and acknowledgement. Put yourself centre stage and, most importantly, have loads of fun.

Well Done...

> For getting to this stage.

> For being you; you haven't lost yourself along the way.

> For all your hard work – make sure you stop, pause and appreciate that.

> For looking after yourself and others in the process.

> For taking up the challenge and for changing things up.

> For all the wins and for all the losses; to try is everything, no matter what the outcome.

CATCHING UP
WITH YOURSELF

To know yourself is everything
To lose yourself is heartbreaking
To find yourself once more is like falling in love
with life all over again

It's important to catch up with friends; find out what they have been up to, what news they have and how they are doing. If we don't, we lose touch, we don't know what is happening in their lives and eventually we grow apart. Maybe we still think they have a horrible boss when they have moved jobs; maybe we don't know they have had a radical new haircut, lost someone close to them or started a new relationship..We approach them from a historical place of knowing and expect them to be as they were, not as they are now.

In the same way, when we go through a lot of change very rapidly, we can lose touch with ourselves. **We can** lose sight of how we have changed, the progress we have made and who we are now.

When we carry on working with a historic version of ourselves - someone we once were - and think we are still 'that person', we can get stuck in a rut, focusing on problems that have actually been resolved or situations that have moved on, and not seeing the new opportunities that are being presented to us. It may be that we have to make sure our plan of action still aligns with our values, for example. We might need to remind the people around us that we are not 'that person' they still think we are. That we have changed.

How can you recognise who you are now?

CHART YOUR PROGRESS

When you are right in it, or 'just after' it, you can't see the progress you have made, so it's easy to see the 'old you' and your 'old life' and think that you're no further forward. Sit down, take yourself back to the beginning of that crisis and write down all the challenges you have faced and exactly what has changed, what you have achieved and how things are different now. I sometimes look back in my diary and see what was going on back then. Put yourself back at that time - how did you feel, how did your life look, what were your prospects or ideas about how your future would pan out? Well, now it's different, and that's down to you.

LET OTHER PEOPLE REMIND YOU

Our friends and family are our best counsels. They are outside the immediacy of the situation, they can be objective, their memories seem to be much more accurate and they can see exactly who we are and where we are now. They can correct our 'historical thinking' and our 'historical identity' and make sure we don't forget our progress.

SHAKE THINGS UP

A night away or a change of scene can really shift our perspective. A bit of sea air, a few days with friends or a couple of days off from our usual environment and the normal humdrum of life can help us reflect and return reinvigorated and clearer about where we are now, what our priorities are moving forward and where we want to focus our energies.

REVISIT THE PAST

Take a brief trip into the past but don't dwell there. Looking back at old photos, historic social media posts or even physically visiting places where you once lived, worked or had significant life moments can help you remember that you are now different. You have moved on.

NOTICE

The most effective way of seeing how far we have come is noticing those moments when we catch ourselves responding in a new way to an old trigger. When we are able to respond rather than react, when we see that we have managed to handle familiar situations in a different way to how we used to and are being rewarded with different results, we know that all the effort we have put in has worked and it has all been worth it.

Have a good catch up with yourself. You will find out things you didn't know, realise what has changed for you, discover more about who you are now and see that it has all been down to you. You've done it. Well done.

LETTING YOURSELF SHINE

You were not put here so your talents and
passion could be squashed
You were born to shine
So, turn your brightness right up
You've changed your world
Now go and change the world

When we change things and become the authority in our own lives, we become more of who we truly are and who we were truly meant to be. **When we bring more of our talents and skills to the world, we can change things for the better and we can help others do the same. We are able to shine.**

For too long we hide our light and don't let ourselves be seen. We don't realise just how long and just how much we have hidden our light until we start to let it shine.

Just as the earth quickly goes from utter darkness

to shimmering light when the sun rises at dawn, when we start letting ourselves shine out in the world **a tiny glimmer suddenly becomes a floodlight.** And it takes just a small step of curiosity to start the process. When you start getting curious about the impact you can make out in the world just by being more of yourself, you won't want to press that dimmer switch ever again.

How can you shine?

DON'T BE AFRAID

We can be afraid of showing who we truly are for fear of being rejected by others, or laughed at or shamed. But the thing that we should all fear much more is that we never allow ourselves to shine and never show who we are truly born to be. That is more terrifying. Choose the lesser fear.

DON'T ASK FOR PERMISSION

Maybe you have been told that you 'shouldn't' shine – that it is arrogant or egotistical and you should be quiet, to be like you always have been, to 'fit in' with everyone else. Or maybe you have been told that it's risky or childish, and you should be sensible, 'grown-up' and live in 'the real world'. These are just a set of beliefs and conditioning that society has dictated. You don't need to live like this or by 'their' rules. **You don't need anyone else's permission to shine. You only need your own.**

Who told you that you were less than others
That you didn't deserve
That you weren't good enough
That you shouldn't be heard or be seen?
Instead of believing them
Show them who you are

SPREAD THE LIGHT

When you make positive changes in your life, it's not unusual for other people around you to start to get curious and ask how you did it, and they may also be motivated to start doing the same. When people see others living their life authentically, they want some of that good stuff too. Shining out in the world has a real ripple effect.

BE AUTHENTIC

You are now more of who you truly are and are making changes in your life that align with your life purpose. They are in resonance and all travelling in the same direction. And this makes their impact off the scale. When you allow yourself to shine, you may find opportunities that match with your purpose and your intentions will arise out of seemingly nowhere. You are being authentic. Life receives this powerful message loud and clear and responds. Each of us has something special to bring to this world. Authentic, positive and powerful things come from authentic, positive and everyday actions.

Spread... your love, kindness and generosity

Share... your lessons learned, your wisdom, your knowledge

Extend... a helping hand, a listening ear, a reassuring glance

Give... your time, your skills, your energy

Radiate... joy, friendship, inspiration, hope

It's not in anyone's interest for you to be off stage, hiding in the wings or out of the spotlight. **Be yourself, take a deep breath, walk centre stage and shine bright for everyone to see. You'll be surprised by how well you already know your lines.**

Every experience will change you

Every day when you wake up you are different

Every night when you go to sleep you are someone else

There's always a new year, a new month, a new day and a new moment

There's always another opportunity

ALWAYS WITH YOU

A good student of life
Looks around, listens carefully, feels their way
And learns from all of it

Life crises, challenges and changes are the ultimate never-ending story. That's life. But there is a difference in how we approach these. We can be sunk by crises, paralysed by challenges and terrified by changes. Or we can rise up, face them and move forward through them. Realising your power, finding your power and knowing your power will help you to do just that. Once you find your power, whatever life throws at you, you'll be able to find it again and you'll be OK. More than OK. **All that you have been through and all that you have learned has unlocked your power and you are in charge now.**

If we truly understand life, then we know that we always have that power inside of us to help us to keep learning, to help us when things change again and to keep us on solid ground. If we think we know everything or that all our changes are done, we are kidding ourselves. If we don't realise that we have the power inside of us at all times to change how we respond to life, we won't grow, or evolve, and we can become pretty rigid in how we view things, shutting ourselves off from new opportunities. Once we do, it gets easier. And, in fact, it can get quite exciting. We realise life is the ultimate adventure fuelled by that power we all have inside us to take us in the direction we want to go.

How to step into your power

RESPECT YOUR TEACHER

Life is the greatest teacher we will ever have. It is only through our experiences that we can really understand, learn and grow. If life keeps giving you the same kind of lesson, respect that it is probably because you haven't learned it well enough the first time. That lesson is still on your own unique syllabus for a reason. Listen, focus and concentrate. We all have subjects and topics that we are 'good' at and others that take a little bit more time.

WORK HARD AND BE CURIOUS

It is not about taking great leaps. It is about taking small, conscious, determined steps on your path. With hard work and a commitment to wanting to learn and change, you will get there. So stick at it. Try to forget outcomes. Be curious instead. An interested approach works better than a pressurised, heavy one. Go with the flow and treat life like a game, like an adventure that you have chosen to be surprised on.

DON'T BE AFRAID TO MAKE MISTAKES

Learning anything takes time, it takes practice, it takes making 'mistakes' and having what we don't want happen, so that we know what we do want. If you take a step back or fall back into those old patterns or habits, don't worry, don't criticise yourself and don't think there wasn't any point in all your efforts. 'Mistakes' are how we learn and evolve. Don't be afraid of making them. Your journey in life is your own and it will happen in its own way and in its own time. Don't compare yourself to others. There is no prescribed timetable.

PUSH YOURSELF

It's tempting to just focus on the subjects that we are already good at and ignore those that we feel unsure of. However, to be a well-rounded and successful student of life, we have to push ourselves to address the hard things and be open to the difficult lessons in all areas of our lives.

TAKE TIME OUT

We need a break from learning and we need time out. Sometimes we think we need to learn everything now or we need to 'fix' ourselves to be good enough. You don't need to 'fix' anything. You are perfect as you are *and* you can learn new things. It's OK to let things settle for a while without having to learn anything new. Relax, take things at the pace that life is presenting things to you. Life knows when you are ready to start a new lesson and when you are not quite there yet. Above all, celebrate your successes and congratulate yourself every time you 'graduate' or get a pass mark in a module.

The best teachers are enthusiastic and have our best interests at heart; they challenge us, believe in us and teach us things that they think would be most useful for us. They don't choose easy lessons or stick to a templated curriculum or let us get away with not doing our home-work. Because they want us to succeed. **Life wants us to succeed too. We are all lifelong learners and our lessons never end.** And that's something we can either feel exhausted by or excited about.

Your power lies in choosing the attitude you take. **You get to decide how your lessons are learned and how your story goes.** That's the power that you have.

YOUR POWER, YOU AND YOUR LIFE

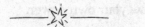

Your power has always been there; it has always
been inside you
Now it's finding its voice
Now it's showing its true self
Now it's letting you know who you truly are,
reflecting back to you who you are becoming and
showing you how your life can be
You have come a long way from sitting back
and watching life just happen *to* you
You've realised that power exists
You've understood what that power is
You've used that power
You've realised that you *are* that power

When life hits hard, your power is the starting point of everything - that trusted, secure and reliable place you can always go to first, before anything else. And you've become more of who you truly are, and more of who you were always meant to be by getting in touch with that place inside yourself. You have overcome and you've become. And that power has transformed your life from something that just happened *to* you, into something that *is* you. Now, you can 'happen' to your life.

Always know your own power.

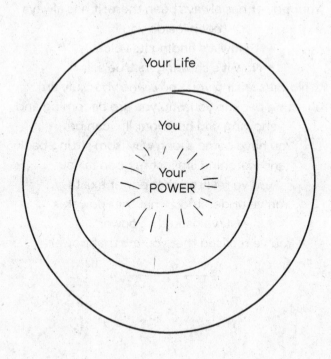

ACKNOWLEDGEMENTS

Huge thanks to Liz Gough for her belief in me and for giving me this incredible opportunity to try to make a difference in the world with this book and, alongside her, Olivia Nightingall and Julia Kellaway for helping me express to the best of my ability what is in my heart. I appreciate you all.

Thank you to all my wonderful friends who have encouraged me, believed in me and supported me, not just with this book, but throughout my life. I have learned so much from all of you and I am so lucky to have you in my life. To Georgina, Rose, Michelle, Jasdeep, Asiya, Susanne, Dan, Lisa, Helga, Jenny, Ali, Ceefee, Katie, Vic, Cathy, Kev and Eve.

I want to express my gratitude to all the incredible people I have encountered in my work who believed in me and gave me the opportunity to use my voice for good, and to all those who have created projects with me to help spread kindness, love and hope.

Thank you to everyone who hasn't believed in me,

every situation that hasn't gone my way and every obstacle that has presented itself. You have helped me to develop even more drive and determination, and given me an even stronger sense of purpose to carry on doing what I do, to never give up and to believe in myself.

Thank you to life for all the lessons you have encouraged me to learn, and for all the lessons you keep asking me to learn. I know that every difficult thing I have experienced has provided a word, a sentence and a whole chapter for this book.

Thank you for nature, for music and for movement for never failing to help me through.

All my love and gratitude go to my lovely family. To Gita, for opening the door, to Mike, Charles, Sophia and Georgia. To Ramayana, for the determination, to Jeremy, Hugo, Poppy, Oscar and Archie. To Kush, for the direction and the companionship. Thank you all for your unending love, understanding and kindness.

And to both of my parents and their love. To my dearest mum, for her strength and for being a true role model of resilience, as well as her kindness and gentleness. And to my dearest dad, for his determination and for always being there, as well as his perseverance and his wise words. I'm forever grateful to you both.

And, finally, my immense gratitude to everyone who reads this book, who passes it on to someone who might need it and who tries to live its message of empowerment, love and hope.

books to help you live a good life

Join the conversation and tell
us how you live a #goodlife

🐦 @yellowkitebooks
📘 YellowKiteBooks
📌 Yellow Kite Books
📷 YellowKiteBooks